MaryAnn Gonyea

CATHEXIS READER
Transactional Analysis Treatment of Psychosis

CATHEXIS READER
Transactional Analysis Treatment of Psychosis

JACQUI LEE SCHIFF

in collaboration with

Aaron W. Schiff
Ken Mellor
Eric Schiff
Shea Schiff
David Richman
Joel Fishman
Linda Wolz
Cheryl Fishman
Diane Momb

Harper & Row, Publishers, Inc.
New York   Evanston   San Francisco   London

Cathexis Reader

Copyright © 1975 by Cathexis Institute

All rights reserved. Printed in the United States of America. No part of this book may be used or reproduced in any manner whatsoever without written permission except in the case of brief quotations embodied in critical articles and reviews. For information address Harper & Row, Publishers, Inc., 10 East 53rd Street, New York, N.Y. 10022.

Library of Congress Cataloging in Publication Data

Schiff, Jacqui Lee.
   Cathexis reader.
     Includes bibliographical references and index.
     1. Psychoses. 2. Transactional analysis.
I. Cathexis Institute. II. Title. [DNLM: 1. Psycho-analytic Therapy. 2. Psychoses—Therapy. WM200 S333c]
RC512.S34   616.8'914   75-14327
ISBN 0-06-045773-2

CONTENTS

	Preface	vii
1	Introduction	1
2	Passivity	5
3	Ego States	23
4	Child Development	32
5	Frame of Reference and Redefining	49
6	Pathology	72
7	Reparenting and Regression	88
8	Treatment Philosophy	98

PREFACE

Cathexis Institute is an educational organization with emphasis on research and experimentation in the genesis and treatment of incapacitating psychiatric disturbances. One of the unique characteristics of the organization is the free flow of ideas and observations between patients and staff, and the very active investment of patients in identifying the characteristics and confrontation of those problems we research. We wish to express deep appreciation to all those who have contributed to our understanding.

Although this material was developed over several years, it was mostly written in an intensive write-in weekend. Participants in that weekend were J. Fishman, K. Mellor, A. Schiff, J. Schiff, S. Schiff, T. Steckel, and T. Wilson. All are professional staff members of Cathexis Institute with the exception of A. Schiff, who is on the staff of Rocky Mountain Transactional Analysis Institute.

It was not our purpose to include comprehensive discussion of any of the issues presented. Rather, we hoped to present an outline of our ideas in a form sufficiently coherent to be useful to other professionals, and to protect our copyrights so that we may freely teach these ideas and techniques. It is our expectation that most of the material presented here will be developed further either in book form or in professional publications.

Transactional Analysis is our primary frame of reference, and in the interest of conciseness we have assumed some rudimentary exposure to transactional analysis concepts by our readers. While our major focus is on the treatment of severe (incapacitating) psychiatric disorders, our own experience and the experience of many others utilizing this material has demonstrated the applicability of the theory and techniques to other, less disabling treatment problems. The material has also been extensively utilized with general self-actualizing programs undertaken to enhance or improve autonomous functioning, and by industrial organizations in improving efficiency.

Because of the continuous flow of ideas among staff, trainees, and patients, it is difficult to assign credit for specific parts of the material among the major contributors. However, contributors are listed according to the amount of input utilized here. The passivity material originated with A. Schiff and J. Schiff, who contributed actively to most of the ideas presented. K. Mellor and E. Schiff developed much of the expanded discussion of discounting; J. Schiff is principally responsible for the parenting and child development material; and E. Schiff contributed to the development of regressive techniques and the frame of reference material. K. Mellor and E. Schiff developed the redefining material. J. Fishman, K. Mellor, and S. Schiff have all contributed to other ideas presented here and made specific contributions to the frame of reference data. Linda Wolz contributed to the catatonic material, and C. Fishman and D. Momb to the hysteric material.

Developing this material through several years of group process has often been fun (and sometimes not fun). The sharing and personal growth involved has been uniquely gratifying to all of us, and utilizing the material for the more effective treatment of patients we care about has been a source of ongoing excitement and stimulation.

Jacqui Lee Schiff

Chapter One

INTRODUCTION

Cathexis Institute is an interdisciplinary organization established to bring together professionals interested both in pursuing research into the social, cultural, and psychological origin and psychotherapeutic treatment of severe emotional disturbances, and in training others to utilize the theories and techniques developed. There are presently two programs, in Hollywood and Oakland, California, which are engaged in research utilizing laboratory treatment programs and in training professionals. Additionally, there are many treatment and training centers which are using and expanding the work already done at Cathexis. Though the institute has continued the pioneer work of its founder Jacqui Schiff on the problem of schizophrenia, the theoretical models and treatment techniques developed are applicable to a broader range of problems, such as those encountered in schools, religious communities, organizational structures, and child rearing.

When Moe and Jacqui Schiff took the first schizophrenic youngster into their home in 1965 there was no reason to predict the developments which have occurred. At that stage very little was known about the effective treatment of schizophrenia. Shortly thereafter "the family" had grown to fifteen, and the process of reparenting was begun when experimentation with the de-cathexis of the Parent ego state yielded positive results. During this phase, information was collected about pathological processes and the external structures and interventions needed to successfully treat them. There were both dramatic successes and disappointing failures. The results of this period were published by Jacqui Schiff, Aaron Schiff, and three other family members in the *Transactional Analysis Bulletin,* July 1969. In her article "Reparenting Schizophrenics"[1] Ms. Schiff described the treatment situation of the family, the relinquishing of the children by the natural parents, the establishment of the primary relationship with a new mother, and the initial messages essential to accomplishing this. An essential aspect of the environment was the expectation for undefended relating and the lack of secrecy. The article defined the schizophrenic structure as a locked system of interrelated messages and adaptations in each ego state, discussed what was known about the frames of reference for paranoia, catatonia, and hebephrenia, and noted the selection problem (thinking disorder) common to all the schizophrenics. Regression was recognized as useful therapeutically, but it was still uncertain what kind and how much support was safe, useful, or appropriate. Many points in that article were to be changed or elaborated on in the next phase of development. Aaron Schiff's article describing the process of shifting from pathological adaptations to the old Parent to healthier adaptations to the new Parent (prior to the extensive use of regressive techniques) is likewise incomplete but essentially correct.

The next step is characterized by the development and publication of the theoretical models which integrated the data collected by then, explained some of the failures, and provided the direction for future research. In response to the demands presented by Eric (later to become Eric Schiff), the most regressive patient encountered to that date, the use of regressive techniques was explored and extended far beyond anything which had been tried previously. The reality of the urgent needs of the infant inside each schizophrenic began to be fully recognized. Concurrent with the exploration of the new regressive techniques, intensive examination of the problem of passivity began. There had been certain patients where, despite concerted effort, it had not been possible to interrupt a pattern of passive behaviors. Obviously, the passivity was being reinforced. This research culminated in the publication of the article "Passivity"[2] by Aaron and Jacqui Schiff in which

---

1. "Reparenting Schizophrenics," *Transactional Analysis Bulletin,* Vol. 8, No. 31 (July, 1969).

2. "Passivity," *Transactional Analysis Journal 1,* No. 1 (January 1971).

the structure and dynamics of passivity syndrome were defined in terms of symbiosis (pathological), discounting, grandiosity, and passive behaviors. The article then outlined the treatment approach which had been developed on these theoretical bases. Of course, research into passivity did not end there but has continued, and as more has been learned, both the theory and the treatment have been expanded and modified.

The first in-depth presentation of the research on schizophrenia was the publication of *All My Children*[3] by Jacqui Schiff and Beth Day. The use of regression was explained and expanded as well as the general process of reparenting. For the first time the degree of intimate involvement between the therapist and the patient was discussed. In a psychiatric climate in which touch stroking was considered grossly improper, and transference-and-counter-transference were to be encountered from opposite sides of a desk, the ideas presented in the early literature on reparenting were viewed as outrageous. Controversy over the methods and theory escalated and research had to continue in an atmosphere of antagonism which often threatened the survival of the family. With time controversy has abated. The effectiveness of the techniques and the validity of the theories have been observed and accepted. Others have used them with similar results to those experienced by the Schiffs. Some of the controversy centered on the use of diagnosis and diagnostic categories which were seen as supporting a destructive system of labeling. Researchers at Cathexis have held that if a diagnostic term names an observable syndrome whose genesis and structure are known, a diagnosis becomes a useful therapeutic tool. In a structure where diagnosis is not considered relevent to OKness, it merely defines the set of dynamics and interrelated problems which the patient and therapist may then solve together. Schizophrenia is considered a solvable problem at Cathexis.

As the controversy waned there grew a demand from the professional community for greater access to the research and for training in the methods and techniques of the Schiff family. This shift in focus from treatment to research and training was facilitated by the excitement and energy of the staff at Cathexis. A laboratory outpatient program was developed in response to the requirements for research and training as well as to the obvious need to have diverse treatment struc-

---

3. *All My Children* (New York: M. Evans and Publishing Co., Inc., 1970).

tures beyond the residential program utilized in the earlier stages. In 1971 Cathexis School was opened in Danville, California, for children who were unmanageable in public schools. In 1973 it moved to Oakland, California, to expand its facilities and services. At present this program seems a promising approach and a viable alternative to hospitalization for many people. Vital aspects of the earlier programs have been successfully incorporated in the outpatient structure, particularly the emphasis on undefended relating, lack of secrecy, and a sharing of responsibilities between individual and group which included therapists as members of the group.

Significant new theoretical material is being developed using just the resources already mentioned. The interest in passivity has continued, and work in that direction has been expanded and elaborated. There have been important developments in understanding the concept of "frame of reference" and in exploring and defining specific frames of reference for the thinking involved in pathological associational structures. Another focus of interest has been the ways in which people redefine reality, especially in stressful situations, in order to have a reality with which they are more comfortable and can confront with more confidence in their capacity for problem-solving. A model has been constructed which provides a clear statement of both the roles and dynamics of redefinition. Other areas where theory of major significance have been developed are hysteria, paranoia, hebephrenia, and manic-depressive and obsessive-compulsive disorders.

From an unexpected and tentative beginning in 1965, Cathexis has grown into an organization dedicated to exploring and solving the problems so evident in the field of mental health and debilitating emotional disorders. The goal is cure and the successes thus far indicate that it is an achievable goal. There are at present numerous treatment and training centers utilizing the work of Cathexis, and there is growing international awareness. This adds an important and exciting dimension to the research, from which useful feedback and new ideas are already developing, as well as providing help to many people to whom real help was not previously available.

Cathexis Institute is committed to public and professional education, and to the development of resources in the mental health field that utilize new and creative philosophies of treatment. This compendium is being published to further that goal.

Chapter Two

PASSIVITY

INTRODUCTION

Operating from the assumption that a healthy organism is reactive, a major focus for research has been how people don't do things (respond to stimuli) or don't do them effectively. Passivity in feeling, thinking, or doing disrupts the balance of social functioning and results in internal distress or behavior disorders.

We see passivity as resulting from unresolved dependency (symbiosis). Discounting is the mechanism, and grandiosity (distortions of reality) provides the justification.

SYMBIOSIS

Definition

A symbiosis occurs when two or more individuals behave as though between them they form a whole person. This relationship is characterized structurally by neither individual cathecting a full complement of ego states. While we treat symbiosis as pathological, it is important to keep in mind that every significant relationship will have, at some time, an element of symbiosis. A working knowledge of symbiosis enables a therapist to teach a patient how to function in problem-solving, to utilize the transference in the service of treatment goals, and to make rapid and crisp intervention in transactions.

Healthy Symbiosis

Symbiosis is a natural occurrence between parents and children. From conception until children are mature enough to provide for their own food, clothing, shelter, and strokes, it is necessary for their survival. If this relationship is disruped, a substitute must be supplied.

Eric Berne defined mental health as a capacity for spontaneity, awareness, and intimacy.[4] A symbiosis may promote these capacities when individuals are lacking in information, thinking skills, physical skills, or strokes. Examples of these are infants, who can provide none of these; or physically or intellectually handicapped people in the area of the handicap; or people with a reactive depression.

Unhealthy Symbiosis

A symbiosis becomes pathological when it interferes with the development of the three capacities mentioned. An example of this is the "smothering mother," who constantly showers the infant with "affection." Spontaneity is interfered with because the infant does not have an opportunity to initiate affection. Intimacy is interfered with because offers of affection and acceptance of it are not bilateral. Awareness is interfered with because the infant does not have time and motivation to explore the world. The young child's time and energy is structured by the mother's demand for attention.

In general, symbiosis is dysfunctional when it interferes with survival or gratification. Survival is interfered with, first, by the establishment of a relationship in which each party has only part of the skills or internal structure that are needed. Therefore, a threat to one is a threat to both. Second, each individual's options are limited due to the necessity of protecting the other individual in the symbiosis. Third, the efficiency of solving a problem is limited by having only one view of each issue involved, as opposed to having two views for checks or corroboration. However, in each of these cases survival need not be the specific issue, because the extent to which a person is less competent interferes with gratification. This is an issue as each party is not free to feel independently in a symbiotic relationship.

---

4. Eric Berne, *Games People Play* (New York: Grove Press, 1974), p. 184.

Relationship to Games

Games are attempts to reenact symbiotic relationships that the children did not resolve with their parents, or are an angry reaction to those relationships. The reenactment gives a sense of security. Either the children are in the position of being taken care of or they are the competent caretakers. In the first case they don't have to worry about a problem because it has become someone else's responsibility. In the second case they don't have to worry because it is not their problem any longer. They perceive the problem as belonging to the other party, for whom they are kindly providing assistance.

Games which result from anger at the symbiotic relationship reinforce that relationship by not terminating it. Essentially these people are affirming the symbiotic relationship and reacting to that affirmation with anger. This is an attempt to shift responsibility for resolving the symbiotic relationship to the other parties in the game.

Symbiotic relationships can be viewed either structurally or functionally. The appropriateness of which view should be utilized in analysis is dependent on the problem being analyzed.

Structural

The relationships which result from a symbiosis are either competitive or complementary. In a competitive symbiotic relationship each

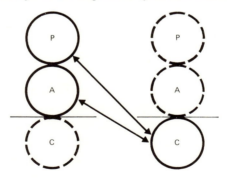

Example:

Mother: "Johnny, I know that it's hard for you to get along with your brother, but you should at least try."

Johnny: "But mom, I've been trying and I just can't stand him."

FIG. 1. Complementary Symbiosis

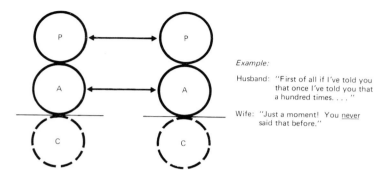

FIG. 2. *Competitive Symbiosis*

party is competing for the same position in the symbiosis, e.g., dependent child. (See Fig. 2) In this case there will often be an escalation of anger, agitation, incapacitation, etc. In a complementary relationship both parties agree as to their mutual positions. (See Fig. 1) The point of the escalation in a competitive relationship is to define which party will get the position which is deemed most favorable by both once the complementary relationship is established.

In a first order structural symbiosis the relationship is one in which both parties either exclude whole ego states or discount some aspect of an ego state. They either relate from contaminations or with exclusions.

In the competitive example both perceive the position of defining reality as preferable. Eventually one will give in or they will discontinue the relationship.

Second order structural symbiosis is more disabling than first order symbiosis. Any of the above patterns may apply and each pattern is established in infancy. For example, if mothers make demands of their children to meet their needs, the infants' view may be that in order to survive they must meet their mothers' needs. This can lead to an accelerated development of A_1 and P_1. (See Chapter Five Schizophrenic Frame of Reference.) The pattern of this type of symbiosis initially occurs as in Figure 3.

Functional

Functional symbioses occur when people decide that function is more important than ego states. This can be either mild or severe. Male

Passivity 9

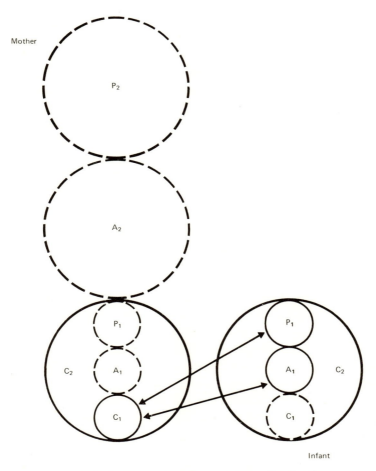

FIG. 3. Example of Second Order Symbiosis

and female sex roles scripting is a mild variation, e.g., "As the man of this house I should stay out of the kitchen, and as the woman you should stay out of the workshop." This can translate as "I can use my Adult in the workshop, but not the kitchen. You can use your Adult in the kitchen but not in the workshop." A manic-depressive family structure is an extreme variation. (See Chapter Six, Manic-Depressive Frame of Reference).

Intervention

It is important to keep in mind that symbiotic relationships are labile. Positions, roles, and the symbiotic contract are often in flux. The intensity of a symbiosis changes with the degree of threat perceived and with the confidence of the individuals that they can successfully deal with the problems facing them.

Understanding the function of a symbiosis is vital to successful treatment. The primary maneuver is aimed at shifting responsibility for a problem to another person or other people. After careful analysis of the game and the symbiotic problems which generate it, the therapist must decide whether the contract goal would be most efficiently reached by: (1) accepting the symbiosis and working with it, (2) confronting it, (3) or interrupting it by shifting the problem back to the patient.

PASSIVE BEHAVIORS

We have identified four passive behaviors people use to establish unhealthy symbiotic relationships. They are (1) doing nothing, (2) over-adaptation, (3) agitation, and (4) incapacitation or violence. These behaviors are the external manifestations which accompany the internal mechanism and processes of discounting, grandiosity, and thinking disorders to be discussed. The use of any one of the passive behaviors is an attempt to establish a symbiosis, and any response to them is necessarily symbiotic. In treatment the aim is to react to the behavior so that the patients respond actively and so that the therapist can move out of the symbiosis as quickly as possible. Active behavior involves thinking, feeling, and acting autonomously. Without discounting, the patients establish separate goals, figure out how to reach them, think about what they are doing, and do it.

Definition

The passive behaviors are the internal as well as the external actions people employ to avoid autonomous response to stimuli, problems, or options, in order to meet their needs or reach goals within the structure of unhealthy symbiotic relationships.

Doing Nothing

Doing nothing involves a nonresponse to stimuli, problems, or options. Rather than the patients' energy being channeled into action, it is utilized to inhibit responses. While doing nothing, patients are usually aware of being uncomfortable and of their own identity, but they do little thinking about what is happening.

Example: Bill says to Jerry, "I'm mad about your being late." Jerry looks scared and does not respond. As he waits for a response Bill gets increasingly uncomfortable and may have impulses to rescue (i.e., ask "What were you doing?") or persecute.

Overadaptation

When people overadapt they do not identify their own goals but accept other people's stated goals or fantasize what these goals are without thinking about their relevance or significance. Because overadapted people frequently seem so obliging, overadaptation often gets a lot of reinforcement from others. Overadaptation is contrasted to adaptation in which the people think about and set their own goals in relation to a realistic assessment of the situation. This is the most difficult passive behavior to identify. However, it is the most amenable to treatment, since overadapted people can be given a great deal of objective information about their abilities, capacities, the situation, and the consequences of their behavior. This procedure confronts their discounting in a way which makes it very difficult for them to continue to discount. In addition, of the four passive behaviors, overadaptation is the one in which the most thinking occurs. This can be used in the service of moving the people to adaptation through statements made from Parent or Adult such as, "You can think," "You can act effectively," "You can decide on your own goals," and "You can solve problems."

Examples: (1) Joe has decided to go to the store to do some shopping. Just as he is leaving he is asked (or told) to mow the lawn which he does immediately without a word. (2) Mary is making a show of having difficulties carrying packages, and Jane takes some of them from her without being asked.

One method for confronting overadaptation is to present the patients with unreasonable or even ridiculous expectations in an attempt to get them to utilize their own Adult to define what is appropriate and what is not appropriate; this will probably result in an externalization of anger and will break down symbiosis.

Agitation

Agitation involves people engaging in repetitive, non-goal-directed activity. It is characterized by the agitated individuals experiencing a very uncomfortable tingling sensation; the activity is meant to avoid or reduce the sensation. The avoidance behaviors are used to work up energy. Thinking is confused and unproductive, and these people are acutely uncomfortable. They are experiencing a threat to symbiosis and know they need to "do something" effective but think they are inadequate. Agitation is often a sign of impending incapacitation or violence and its significance should not be underestimated. The energy is built up to inhibit uncontrolled behavior.

Interrupting the build-up of energy before it is discharged is best achieved with series of calm, firm statements from Parent such as, "Calm down. Sit down. Now think about what is happening," accompanied by physical stroking. This restores overadapted behavior from which the patients can move to adapted but effective action for solving the problem being discounted. During treatment the patients can be trained to cathect their own Parent to achieve this result. The move to overadapted behavior from agitation appears to be a necessary step as it does not seem possible to cathect the patients' Adult while they are agitated.

An interesting occurrence relevant to agitation is that people experience the sensation of agitation differently. Many, perhaps the majority of people, report that agitation is a specific "electric" or "crawly" sensation which they experience as a tingling response on the skin. Others only experience agitation behaviorally. It appears that agitation is an orally-derived behavior, and for some individuals the agitation is utilized as the shifted feeling. The agitated behavior, in those instances, is used to deny and shift the feelings to someone else. The person picking up the feelings does not experience anger, fear, or guilt. This problem seems to have derived from a decision during the oral stage when the infant experiences the nurturing person as agitated and learns to escalate the agitation as a control mechanism. It tends to be associated with masochistic structures. We have not yet done much work with treating the problem with this view of the mechanism, but would anticipate treatment to consist of getting the individual in touch with the primary sensation. It would be important to make sure the Adult is aware that it is not necessary for anyone to be continuously agitated, as the Child's experience may be that all social relating involves shifts of agitation, and that the person can function adequately while experiencing the sensation.

Examples: (1) Repetitive body movement such as finger tapping, (2) Pacing the floor, (3) Stuttering and stammering, (4) Smoking, and (5) Repetitive thinking.

Incapacitation or Violence

Incapacitation or violence is the discharge of energy built up while people are being passive. At a point of perceived or actual breakdown in the symbiosis, it is an attempt to enforce it. No thinking occurs during the discharge, and the individuals accept no responsibility for the behavior.

With violence, intervention consists of containing the escalation until the energy is discharged. Afterwards the therapists move into rescripting the patients. Generally, we have found no way of cathecting patients Adults until after the discharge has ended. However, with patients who have incorporated new Parent, a stimulus that successfully cathects their Parent will stop the escalation and open the way for Adult cathexis. Especially after the energy discharge has run its course, the patients are likely to be highly available to work. They will have a lot of Child cathected, and their Adult will be easily cathectable. At this point, the patients are expected to take responsibility for the inappropriate behavior and are given information about the dynamics and consequences of the escalation as perceived by others. An important aspect of violence is that the stroking takes place externally—others do or have stroked the patients for the behavior. Changing the patients stroke economy around the behavior is significant; for example, giving negative instead of positive strokes.

When patients escalate incapacitation, they are using an overadapted form of violence. During the escalation there is usually a lot of self-stroking which helps to maintain it, and after the escalation there is likely to be an unwillingness to think about it. The best technique for inducing the patients to think about and take responsibility for the escalation of incapacitation appears to be the withdrawal of support and refusal to take care of them when they incapacitate. By removing the external source of strokes and undercutting the symbiotic pay off the patients are then much more likely to take responsibility for the behavior.

Examples: Incapacitation—fainting, migraine headaches, and vomiting. Violence—physical assault on people or property.

Since people learn to be passive in their families, identifying the nature of the behavior and its likely origins can provide direct access to the nature of their early relationship and the developmental stage at which they were first adopted.

DISCOUNTING

Definition

Discounting is an internal mechanism which involves people minimizing or ignoring some aspect of themselves, others, or the reality situation. Our position is that there is a consensually definable reality, and that discounting involves a frame of reference which distorts or is inconsistent with that reality. By discounting, people can maintain and reinforce a dysfunctional frame of reference, play games, and further their scripts, while attempting to enforce or confirm symbiotic relationships with others. Discounting is not operationally observable. However, we can see such external manifestations of discounting as passive behaviors, redefining transactions, ulterior transactions, and behaviors from positions in the Karpman Drama Triangle.[5] It is important to bear in mind that these external manifestations issue from discounting, but are not discounts themselves.

Classification of Discounts

Discounts have been classified as to area, type, and mode. The three areas people discount are themselves, others, and the situation. In any of these areas, three *types* of discounting may be identified: discounting stimuli, problems, and/or options. Denial of feelings, for example, might be classified as:

---

5. Karpman, S.B., "Fairy Tales and Script Drama Analysis," *Transactional Analysis Bulletin 7,* No. 26 (April 1968).

Area discounted—Self
Type of discount—Stimulus.

There are four modes in which each type of discounting may occur.
1. The *existence* of stimuli, problems, or options are themselves discounted. For example, ignoring pain involves a discount of the stimulus itself. Similarly, some people might discount the very existence of a problem, or the existence of any options to solve a problem or reach a goal.
2. The *significance* of a stimulus, problem, or option may be discounted. Here, some individuals may recognize a stimulus, problem, or option, but minimize or misinterpret its importance or relevance to the situation, self, or others.
3. The *change possibilities* related to stimuli, problems, and options may be discounted. Accordingly, there may be a discount of the *changeability* of stimuli, e.g., "I'm always hungry (internal stimulus); it's genetic"; the *solvability* of problems may be discounted, e.g., "People can't work when they're crippled"; and the *viability* of options may be discounted, e.g., "You just can't talk when you're angry."
4. That some *person* (self or others) can do something different or effective may be discounted. That is, individuals may discount their own ability or someone else's ability to *react differently* to stimuli, to *solve* problems, or to *act on* options.

From Table One, three relationships have been identified.

1. Generally, for each type of discounting, a discount in any of the four modes involves discounts in all those below it on the chart. For example, people who discount a stimulus generally also at the same time discount the significance of the stimulus, the changeability of the stimulus, and their ability to react differently to the stimulus. (See vertical arrow on the table).
2. Generally in any row on the table the discount of a type involves discounts of all types to the right. For example, people who discount pain (stimulus) will discount the existence of a problem as well as the existence of options to solve the problem around the pain.
(See horizontal arrow on the table.)

TABLE 1. *Relationships Between Types and Modes of Discounting*

MODE	TYPE OF DISCOUNTING		
Existence	T_1 Existence of Stimuli	T_2 Existence of Problems	T_3 Existence of Options
Significance	T_2 Significance of Stimuli	T_3 Significance of Problems	T_4 Significance of Options
Change Possibilities	T_3 Changeability of Stimuli	T_4 Solvability of Problems	T_5 Viability of Options
Personal Abilities	T_4 Person's Ability to React Differently	T_5 Person's Ability to Solve Problems	T_6 Person's Ability to Act on Options

3. Discounting occurring at any point on the table also involves discounting in the row below it in the type to the left, and in the row above it in the type to the right (See diagonal arrows on table). For example, if a mother discounts the significance of a baby's crying (stimulus) by shutting the door to the baby's room, she is also discounting the existent problem for the baby. Similarly, if the mother said, "The baby always cries; there's nothing that can be done," she is discounting her own and the baby's ability to react differently to stimuli, discounting the solvability of the problem, and discounting the significance of options. ("It won't make any difference.")

Generally, children raised in environments where discounting is consistently in or near the upper left corner of Table One develop the most incapacitating pathology.

Discounting and Thinking

All discounts are beyond awareness and impair effective thinking. They involve the people thinking in a contamination or with an exclusion. These limit Adult functioning. The limitations are especially apparent in the integration of internal and external processes. The individual playing a game will be unable to deal with a particular issue under discussion by describing:

1. My relevant feelings, thoughts, and actions.
2. Other's relevant feelings, thoughts, and actions.
3. The relevant aspects of the reality situation.

This type of selection problem will always appear when individuals play games. There is necessarily an identifiable discount and a consequent exaggeration in some other aspect of relevance. Identification of the internal mechanism typically used by these people is diagnostically useful in establishing treatment programs.

Treatment Interventions

Whenever a discount is confirmed by an environmental response, a game ensues. Treatment, therefore, is designed to confront discounting in a directional stepwise manner. The general direction in treatment is from external to internal and then to an integration of both considerations, though this should not be considered a rigid schedule. Treatment begins by helping the patients identify the external manifestations, such as the transactions, behaviors, and games that issue from their discounting. The second step is to focus on the areas, types, and modes of discounting; the focus here being on internal dynamics. The patients' investment in the discounting can then be identified, as a third step, with a view to their de-investing in the discounting behavior. The final step involves these individuals consolidating their investment in behaving and transacting without discounting, and experiencing postive reinforcement from the consequences of their own behaviors. The internal-external integration occurs here.

Therapeutic interventions used during each of the above four steps can be planned to preclude an intervention falling on or below any diagonal indicated on the chart. If the intervention is not above the diagonal along which these people are discounting, the intervention itself is likely to be discounted. Thus, the focus of treatment tends to move from the top left corner of the table to the bottom right corner, focusing on each diagonal as a phase in treatment. Treatment phases are indicated on the table by the inset T's. Each phase has characteristic issues that may need to be dealt with.

T_1: awareness (internal or external)
T_2: significance of awareness, problem definition
T_3: awareness of change (general), defining problem significance, awareness of and defining related options
T_4: awareness of personal abilities for change, defining problem solutions, selection of possible options for action
T_5: awareness of personal problem-solving ability (action options), selection of viable options
T_6: awareness of personal action potential, action itself.

These issues range from awareness of aspects of the self, others, or the reality situation, through thinking about that awareness in order to define problems and options to solve them, to acting effectively on those options. Discounting, grandiosity, or thinking disorders may interfere at any stage and will need to be dealt with when they occur.

GRANDIOSITY

Definition

Grandiosity is an internal mechanism involving an exaggeration (maximization or minimization) of some aspect of the self, others, or the situation. For example, the statement, "I was so scared I couldn't think," involves a maximization of the significance of the feeling, as well as a minimization of the person's abilities to think when scared.

Functions of Grandiosity

Grandiosity is used by people to justify the maintenance of the symbiosis. For example, if an individual's frame of reference precludes thinking when scared, then the solution to the problem is expected to come from the environment (rescue). Further, grandiosity compensates for these individual's perception of themselves as inadequate. If "scared to death," these people avoid dealing with fears related to their inadequacy to cope with the situation at hand. The thinking underlying grandiosity involves a delusional "I can't stand it" position and effects a shift of responsibility to others and/or the situation.

THINKING DISORDERS

Internal and External Processes

Eric Berne's definition of healthy functioning as spontaneous, aware, and intimate[6] describes an individual who has accomplished a functional integration of internal and external processes. Internal processes are those activities which go on inside the individual's head. External processes are the behavioral integration of the individual with the environment. Awareness refers to Adult analysis of oneself in relationship to the environment. Spontaneity safely occurs when the individual can anticipate interference from the Adult and Parent should the spontaneous reaction be ill-advised. Intimacy requires a value structure where it is possible to relate to parts of the external environment (people and situations) from a position of trust and vulnerability. Disorders occur when people operate primarily from either an internal frame of reference, or try to adapt totally to external situations without reference to internal frame of reference, or when interpretation of data is atypical, making difficult an alliance between what is internal and what is external.

Examples: Individuals who are overadapted or excessively competitive utilize an excessive emphasis on the external situation; individuals who are self-centered or rebellious function from an internal frame of reference; and individuals whose learning has provided them with unique definitions of either internal or external activity will be unable to integrate the two.

A major manifestation of malfunctioning in thinking about internal and external processes will be demonstrated around the structuring of time and goals. When there is an overemphasis on external situations, there will be problems with motivation, since in that case activity is only indirectly integrated with feeling. An internal frame of reference will result in ineffective assessment of external reality, and accom-

---

6. Berne, *Games People Play.*

plishing goals will become difficult in relation to omitted or distorted views of situations. The individuals with misinformation will experience confusion in the areas of misinformation when they try to relate to others and are likely to give up in order to avoid the sensation of being overwhelmed. For example, individuals who do not experience somatic hunger are likely to not understand it and are thus unable to share social activities related to the gratification of eating. They may, as a result of anxiety, withdraw from eating activities, or eating may become an agitated behavior, resulting in overeating.

Selection Problems

The difficulty in integrating data into meaningful thinking structures is generally demonstrated as a difficulty in selecting relevant data and integrating this data into a functional gestalt. As thinking becomes more dysfunctional, it appears that a significant focus for the mechanism of the disturbance is bridging the corpus callosum and nonintegration of the two parts of the brain. There seems to be an identifiable relationship between cerebral dominance and those processes which will be excluded in the service of the pathology. (See Chapter 7)

Overdetailing

Around any particular problem it is possible to overwhelm oneself with excessive numbers of stimuli, relevant and irrelevant, and incorrectly weight details as to significance. The result is a massively confusing array of details. This is the most common mechanism for ineffective thinking.

Overgeneralizing

Questions such as "What is the meaning of life?" "Who are you?" "Do you really love me?" are typical of overgeneralized thinking. The problem, by its definition, becomes so general that it is overwhelming in its massiveness, logically unanswerable, or semantically meaningless.

Escalations

Games are played at varying levels of payoffs. The significance of each payoff may be internally defined according to how it is meant to be utilized in the service of the script. However, successful involvement in a game is usually dependent upon finding a complementary player. The two players must then establish a mutually satisfactory level of payoff (all without direct discussion of the problem). If one player is reluctant to enter the game at the payoff level desired by the other player, there are likely to be attempts to manipulate or redefine the situation in such a way as to satisfy the player who wants a higher level of payoff.

Example: A marital argument about use of the family car might be escalated into an issue involving separation and divorce. In that case the original problem is no longer the focus of thinking, and appropriate goals get discounted in relation to the original problem.

The escalation may result in a dropout of one of the players for whom the stakes have gotten too high (destructive) for integration into the script. The player who is left can then seek another player. An alternative utilized by psychotic individuals and by some particularly destructive disorders not usually considered psychotic (example: hysteria) is to continue to escalate in a frantic attempt to elicit a response anywhere in the environment.

One of the important utilizations of the discounting materials is to recognize the escalation in the early stages so that intervention is possible before there is a total loss of functioning.

Fantasy

Fantasy is crucial to effective thinking. For example, memory is a fantasy which has been defined as having been real. Anticipation of events to come and easy preparation (structuring) for those events comes out of fantasies. Perceptions involve much fantasizing. For example, in looking at a table from an angle where all four legs are not visible, most of us do not have difficulty identifying the object as a table. We utilize fantasy to define that part of the object which cannot be seen. Much of our conceptualizing, that part of our thinking which comes from Little Professor, is a fantasy structure. The Parent ego state is incorporated as a fantasy.

Disturbances in fantasy are likely to have serious consequences. The person may have difficulty defining reality, may hallucinate, or have delusions, and will certainly have problems with anticipating and planning for future events. Organization becomes overwhelmingly difficult for people who do not have a productive fantasy mechanism available. The utilization of fantasy in the service of thinking can be taught fairly easily; it becomes more difficult to limit fantasy in the service of games.

Genesis of Thinking Disorders

We view thinking as an adaptation which is learned in response to environmental demands. Some individuals, because of biological deficiencies, limitations in environmental stimulation, or exposure to incorrect learning have been unsuccessful in achieving socially functional thinking.

For many people with thinking problems there are script issues which are nearly always accompanied by misinformation, i.e., "Thinking is hard work," or injunctions, i.e., "Think about something else" "Don't worry about it." Often this is accompanied by external problems in the adaptive process caused by excessive parental demands, insufficient demands, or improper demands. We consider effective thinking to be related to a comfortable anal resolution. The Adult begins to operate as an autonomous ego state between the ages of two and three with such a resolution, and the cathexis of the Adult at that stage is structured as a result of the conflict experienced by the children in integrating internal and external demands. When children make a social contract, decide that they are going to share the world with others, they experience a need for integrating much more data into their perceptions. This requires a major step forward in terms of thinking; the resulting pattern provides a set for later thinking (and game playing).

Sometimes the thinking disorder is utilized as a means of avoiding other problems or compensating other problems. Examples are escalating activity, thinking, or feelings as a means of avoidance, or simply never thinking about a particular feeling around which sufficient controls may not exist.

CONCLUSION

The passivity material provides a conceptual framework for dealing with most treatment problems and has proved useful in various other situations. The demand for activity, involvement, and problem-solving, which is intrinsic to the utilization of this material, facilitates effective social functioning in most contexts.

Chapter Three

EGO STATES

INTRODUCTION

Patients with incapacitating psychological disturbances have developed internal structures which do not enable them to integrate internal and external experiences in functional ways. Curing schizophrenia and other severely disabling disturbances is not possible without a model which enables both the therapist and patient to integrate diverse feelings, thoughts, impulses, inhibitions, and values into a clearly understandable gestalt. Structural analysis provides us with that model.[7]

The model has, however, greater ramifications for treatment. The selective manipulation of whole ego states, attention to the energy resources available to individuals in their utilization of ego states, and control of the contents of ego states through environmental reinforcement causing the development of new conditioned responses provide us with major strategies for intervention.

Characteristics of Ego States

The Parent ego state contains definitions of the world, the Child, and the Child's relationship to the world. (*Example:* "You're going to be the best card player in the world.") It gives prescriptions and advice. (*Example:* "Scared money never wins.") It demands action or enjoins actions. (*Example:* "Don't just stand there! *Do* something!") It also contains rules and programs for accomplishing certain tasks. (*Example:* "In order to solve a problem you first have to define it.")

---

7. Berne, E., *Transactional Analysis in Psychotherapy* (New York: Grove Press, 1961), Part I.

The Adult ego state is a data processor and data bank. It uses the Parent's structure for solving problems. It is not self-cathecting. Only when the Parent or Child requests that the Adult think about something does it do so. Most people keep their Adult functioning to some extent all of the time. This is because thinking is a primary survival adaptation.

The Parent and the Adult are both adaptations. They are structured out of the external environment and are subject to cultural influence. They enable the individual to store and select data and make it possible to pursue long-range goals when there is a conflict between the pursuit of the long-range goals and obtaining immediate gratification.

The Child is experienced by healthy persons as the most real part of their personalities. It contains all of the experiences that people have had. It is also the storehouse for the games which he learned from his parents. The Child is the most clever ego state. It's primary concern is how to maximize gratification or comfort and minimize discomfort.

Development and Incorporation of the Ego States

Between birth and six or eight months of age, we have seen three categories of phenomena. The first are reflexive reactions to stimuli, both internal (hunger-crying) and external (being placed against a breast —nuzzling). Second are preferences or avoidances that seem intrinsic to a particular experience (not liking strained carrots). Third are preferences or avoidances which are conditioned. (Crying is extinguished as a reaction to hunger in a pre-hebephrenic infant). These functional phenomena correspond to C_0, A_0, and P_0 (in that order) in Berne's "Standard Structural Nomenclature."[8] At this age children experience internal events and external reality to the extent that an external event makes immediate contact with them. Third order structure (See Fig. 4) becomes useful in conceptualizing motivation. It can be used to trace the various steps of interaction of the ego states back to Natural Child. Thus, P_2 may say, "Boys don't act afraid," A_1 may adapt by escalating anger over fear, but the purpose of all that is to take care of fear as experienced in A_0.

---

8. Berne, E., "Standard Nomenclature," *Transactional Analysis Bulletin 8*, No. 32 (October 1969): 111-112.

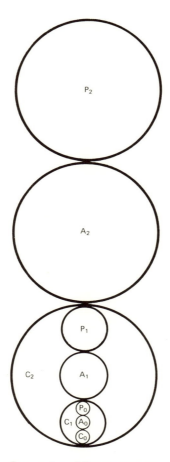

FIG. 4. Development and Incorporation of Ego States

The rest of the personality develops from C_1. A_1 and P_1 begin to develop in infants as they learn to manipulate the social and material world during the mid-infancy period. A_2 begins to function between the ages of two and three years with the parents' demand on the children that they do things they are not motivated to do. In order to accomplish these tasks they must learn to think objectively about them. P_2 is first externalized as an autonomous structure between the ages of nine and ten. This is an attempt to defend the fantasy of their parents which children maintain in P_1 and with which they control behavior.

Example: Four-year-old Johnny says: "My mother doesn't let me do that." Since this is not very potent, Johnny learns by the time he gets to be nine or ten to say, "You shouldn't do that! Stop it!"

Cathexis

The Child ego state is the source of all energy and is in control of cathexis. Much of the content of the Child is adaptations, while the entire contents of the Adult and Parent ego states are adaptations. Psychopathology can be thought of as the development of adaptations which control the Child as opposed to the Child controlling the adaptations.

The function of these adaptation is to promote survival. The Parent defines frame of reference, culture, and values for the Child. The Adult processes data within the frame of reference at the request of the Child or Parent. For some people in some situations the Parent and Adult either contribute nothing to survival (and thereby waste any energy that they may be given) or are direct threats to the survival of the Child.

Example: Four-year-old Johnny cries out in the night that there is a tiger under his bed. Father may come in and say, "Let's take a look. See there's no tiger under there. So, you go on back to sleep." From such incidents Johnny picks up a Parent definition that such a fantasy may be real and should be investigated further. Since father (hopefully) knows that there really isn't a tiger under the bed, the energy that he spends looking for it is wasted. The same is true for Johnny when later in life he cannot make an automatic distinction between his fantasies and reality.

Suppose that Johnny's father responds, "Johnny, tigers only live in zoos around here. They don't live under little boys' beds. Go back to sleep." His Parent will define that some things are only fantasies and do not have to be investigated. If Johnny's father is sensitive to this event as a signal of Johnny's needs for strokes from him, he might structure time so that he and Johnny can relate in gratifying ways.

In a healthy functioning personality the energy distribution may be operationally thought of as in Figure 5, give or take 5%.

Neither the Parent nor the Adult can alone inhibit the Child from doing what it wants or influence it to do what it doesn't want to do.

Only when the Parent and Adult agree on a course of action and combine energies, can the Child be overruled. This may occur through independent assessment or through contamination. The Child's only option in this case would be either to contaminate the Adult in order to override the decision, or to withdraw energy from the other two ego states. This withdrawal of energy can be through either exclusion or decathexis.

Contamination

All people contaminate their Adults with either Parent or Child at times. In severe disturbances these contaminations are especially significant in the energy distribution. Using the percentages given in Figure 5 as a base to work from, it is possible to trace major changes in a

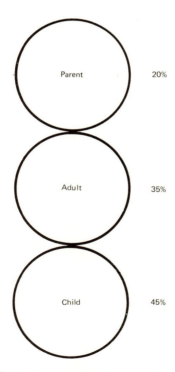

FIG. 5. Energy Distribution Between Ego States

person's behavior based on contamination. The following example is of a boy who left home to go to college and became diagnosably schizophrenic during the first year.

When he was at home his mother and father structured the household rigidly. His clothing, food, and time structuring were all taken care of by the family. He had to act pleasantly, not think about being angry, never act anger out, and get good grades. In this aberrant environment his ego states were functional in their alignment. However, he did experience some lack of stability any time he was away from home. When he arrived at college he didn't have his parents to rigidly structure his life, so he began to use his Parent ego state to do it for him. In order to exercise this control and censor the "evil in the world" and his own not-OK impulses, which his parents censored at home, he had to use a Parent contamination.

At this point it became a threat to his internal structure if he even though about being angry about the rigidity with which he had to live, so he didn't think about it. In about six months his Child got tired of rigid functioning, had collected enough angry stamps, and decided to cash them in. This was done by contaminating his Adult with his Child and was the beginning of a battle for control between his Parent and his

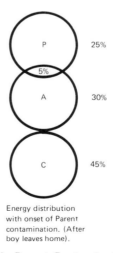

Energy distribution with onset of Parent contamination. (After boy leaves home).

FIG. 6. Parent Contamination

Child. His Parent was saying, "The only way to survive is to be good (do what I say)," and his Child was saying, "The only way that I can survive is if I have my feeling." These were not viewed as reconcilable, but as mutually exclusive. At this point his Adult became useless as an independent data processor. External stimuli were only dealt with from the point of view of their consequence to his precarious internal structure.

Exclusions

Another possible solution to this young man's dilemma would have been to exclude his Parent. The exclusion of an ego state is usually a tactic of desperation. However, it is a common spontaneous solution in relation to an ego state which threatens the survival of the organism, and in a treatment environment which includes reparenting as an option, it is a viable prescription. Parent exclusion also takes place when a person is opting for the Child position in a symbiosis. When this is the case the exclusion may clear up spontaneously if no one is willing to enter the symbiosis. It is important to distinguish between this reason for a Parent exclusion and the former.

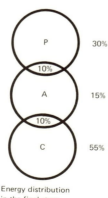

Energy distribution
in the final stage
of a double contamination.
(Boy becomes angry about
internal controls, and ego
states enter conflict for
control of energy).

FIG. 7. Double Contamination

Exclusion of the Adult takes place in three cases. The first is when the individual's Adult is contaminated by the Parent to such an extent that the person finds it difficult to distinguish between the two ego states without external intervention. In this case the exclusion is tied to the exclusion of the Parent. A mild example of this type of exclusion is Scarlet O'Hara's decision in *Gone with the Wind*, "I won't think about it today; I'll think about it tomorrow." If Parent exclusion is decided upon as a therapeutic procedure, it is preferable to decontaminate the Adult first. However, in some cases it works better to initiate the exclusion to whatever extent the two ego states can be separated, in order to reduce internal conflict. The second type of Adult exclusion occurs when the person has a clear injunction against thinking; e.g., "It's not nice to think about such things," or "Don't think! Do it!" In this case the parents have defined thinking as being outside the list of options in a particular situation. The third case again involves an attempt to set up a symbiosis in which the other party becomes responsible for a problem because that person is doing the thinking. This occurs in such games as, "Gee, You're Wonderful Professor," and "Stupid."

Exclusion of the Child is dynamically more complicated than exclusion of the other ego states. In order for this to be done the Child ego state being excluded must support it. With the other ego states this is not necessary. The decision to exclude the Child ego state is based on the conclusion that the source of a problem is having feelings. The Child believes that survival depends on not having these feelings. In treatment this is a very volatile issue. Usually these people will have few or no socially acceptable options for their feelings; for example, the person whose only behavioral option for anger is homocide. In the case of a Child exclusion, it is important that the problem areas be identified and a plan formulated for dealing with them prior to any attempt to break through the exclusion. It is very inadvisable to break down an exclusion without precautions and follow-up.

Decathexis

Decathexis of an ego state is distinctly different from an exclusion. Exclusion involves the withdrawal of unbound cathexis. Decathexis involves the withdrawal of both bound and unbound cathexis.[9] It is only

---

9. Berne, *Transactional Analysis in Psychotherapy*, Chapter 3.

possible to decathect the Child ego state by deciding to die; e.g., classical Buddist monks who sent out notices of their own death. Decathexis of the Adult is also a very rare occurrence. This is because the Adult is very intimately connected with the Child. It is first cathected as an independent ego state between the ages of two and three and usually is part of the persons identification of self; e.g., Descartes' "I think, therefore I am."

Decathexis of Parent is another matter. The Parent is experienced by many people as being external to themselves. Among schizophrenics it is often characterized as another entity in their heads with which they must do battle. In this last case decathexis is not only possible but is often spontaneous.

Conclusion

With any person in whom contaminations or exclusions are extensive, or in whom decathexis has taken place or is likely, it is vital that the consequences of any change in cathexis be given serious consideration. Moreover, treatment plans must take into account the volatile energetic reaction which is always possible when a pathological homeostasis within and between ego states is disturbed.

Chapter Four

CHILD DEVELOPMENT

INTRODUCTION

The function of parenting is to rear a healthy child to maturity and independence. Necessary to accomplishing this task is the formulation of a healthy symbiosis followed by the step-by-step resolution of that symbiosis at a rate consistent with the child's biological and social functioning and the demands of the environment in which that child lives.

Parenting

Certainly the first responsibility for parents is to protect their children from physical threat to their survival or healthy development. At a primitive level that means seeing to it that they have food, warmth, and shelter. Since children are, for some time, incapable of anticipating future events or planning for long-range goals, parents serve these functions in relation to many aspects of physical welfare, such as nutrition, exercise, and medical and dental care. The activity of the parents in those areas will be incorporated into the Parent of the children as "Take care of yourself" and "You are important" messages, and also into the Child as habit training. As children grow older they assume increasing responsibility for those functions which require advanced planning, and their effective accomplishment of them is an indication of their autonomy and awareness of their worthiness.

Facilitation of their children's social functioning is another parental responsibility. Throughout the period of maturation there are identifiable tasks in social learning which are most consistent with a child's biological maturation and the demands of the social environment. If these tasks are not successfully accomplished at the prescribed age, the later awareness of the deficiency and the eventual resolution or non-resolution of the problem is likely to be costly in terms of energy resources, the developmental tasks at hand at that time, and a child's OKness.

In a newborn infant, the ego states can be visualized as empty spaces. As the infant observes, learns, and grows, the spaces are filled up. To a large extent the parents influence what messages, definitions and ideas will be incorporated into each ego state (frame of reference). It is advisable that parents be aware of their goals for their children and that the goals be thoughtfully constructed in view of the anticipated requirements for healthy functioning in relation to both internal and external demands.

A sensible, consistent parent structure is needed to provide adequate protection, not only for the child's physical welfare, but also to establish a climate in which the child can safely grow, test limits, and experience maximum development of spontaneity and creativity. There needs to be opportunity for intimacy and also for separateness, confidence in capacity for solving problems, and confidence in the OKness of outside people and the extended social environment.

Important messages for every child to incorporate are:

1. You can solve problems.
2. You can think.
3. You can do things.

At every stage stroking is important. Children need to experience both positive and negative strokes. At the end of the symbiosis the total should be significantly positive, but during particular developmental stages negative strokes may be more consistently appropriate. Even in those instances, a child gets positive strokes from the parents' investment and involvement. After the oral stage it is important that stroking be somewhat conditional, i.e., relevant to the external as well as the internal aspect of the child, in order to facilitate social awareness, and also to ensure that the child has a secure awareness of the parents' unconditional caring.

A frequent mistake in parenting occurs when the children are not offered enough "what to do" messages. Almost inevitably children will incorporate "don't" messages. However, they may lack the capacity to use these messages without prescriptive messages concerning socially acceptable options for behavior. An overabundance of "don't" messages will not facilitate effective functioning and is most likely to result in agitation. A good rule to practice is, whenever children are told what not to do, they should also be told what to do. This will build their confidence in their own OK-ness and capacity to solve problems, will establish a structure for testing limits, and will teach thinking.

It is important that the parent be potent. Children need to have a parent in their head which can make them do things they don't want to do, and which will prevent them from doing things they should not do. The verbal "shoulds" can only provide a set-up for children to be not-OK if they know what those "shoulds" are and are unable to accomplish them. However, as children grow up, they must take responsibility for making themselves do the "right" thing and test out doing the "wrong" thing. The parents must be sufficiently flexible to permit the child to do that and respond with appropriate positive or negative stroking.

DEVELOPMENTAL STAGES

Pre-natal

Probably the most crucial events during this period are what happens with the parents. For many families a pregnancy is a period of stress. At a time when parents need to be building up a reservoir of strokes to be available for the nurturing needs of the child, external pressures are likely to create a situation where there is a scarcity of strokes, reduction in social contacts, and reduced awareness of the parents' own Child needs.

It is important that the parents not discount their own comforts, worries, and ambivalences during the pre-natal period. As long as the parents stay reactive to stress and actively seek resolution for their discomforts, the likelihood of their being available to establish a healthy symbiosis with the infant is increased. The most damaging circumstances we have seen are those in which one or both of the parents start suppressing feelings, and the child is born into a climate where a major characteristic is lack of responsiveness in the Child ego states of the parents. This results in nurturing being undertaken from a Parent-programmed, not-OK position.

For infants, probably the most significant experiences of this period are the experiences with rhythms. The children experience the rhythms of their own body and also those of their mother's body. This awareness of rhythms and the security and comfort which associate the rhythms to the pre-natal environments, are important in the development of structure at later ages and provide an ongoing resource for gratification and reassurance.

Birth

People who reenact birth either in regressions or with hypnosis, do not ordinarily report experiencing the birth as painful. The strangeness of the experience is frightening. The unexpected slipping away of structure and rhythms at the moment of actual birth provides an association of the sensations which we call fright with a loss of structure, an event over which the individual has no control. Choking and difficulties with breathing in the first few moments of life are experienced by the child as a desperate attempt to reestablish those rhythms (or some rhythms) which will signal restoration of comfort and security.

First Six Months

The most significant thing which happens in the first few months of the life of infants is that they discover that they exist. They learn that there is part of the world which they *are*, and part which they *are not*. For awhile, as they discover their extremities, the part which they *are* seems to be expanding and they reach the termination of this stage believing that it is likely that their being will continue to expand to take in more of their environment. However, already they are beginning to discover limitations imposed on their activity from external sources, and they are puzzled and offended at these.

Rhythms continue to have major importance and to be the source of security; crying, sucking, rocking, and their mother's and their own breathing reinforce this association. However, some nonrhythmical experiences begin to have meaning, and these signal the beginning formation of the symbiosis. The first such nonrhythmical experiences to have significance are awareness of the mother's smell, eyes, and smile. Also, some of these activites which began as rhythms and occurred as reflexes, for example, crying and sucking, start to be influenced by social learning. By the time children are three to five months old, many behaviors are purposeful, in that they are meant to produce specific responses from the external environment. The infants have patterns of reponses associated to the behaviors, and what they experience is that their activity produces the desired responses (when it does). This provides the first associations with doing things and problem solving and lays the foundation for the script in these areas.

When the rhythmical behaviors do not produce the desired results, they are likely to escalate for a period of time; this pattern lays the framework for those behaviors which we later call agitation. The early development of this behavior explains the poor quality of thinking and the inability to cathect Adult in persons who are agitated; the Child is cathected at an age too young to utilize Adult.

The association between the sensation of hunger (internal stimuli), the activity of crying and flailing and sucking (the behavioral bridge between the internal and the external), and the acquisition of food (external response) is crucial. It is the first step in the child's learning to think, the initial step in the script about the significance of activity. It is the beginning source for many incorporated messages about stress, the utilization of energy, and the decision of whether to trust the world. It is likely at a later stage to be translated into a basic position regarding the OKness of the self and the Child's needs.

Things which can go wrong:
1. Overresponsiveness, which requires that the children put out minimal energy, does not help them develop frustration tolerance.
2. Overfeeding results in discomfort associated with gratification.
3. Nonassociation of hunger to gratification of eating. This is likely to occur in some handicapped children, or children born prematurely, especially if tube fed. It will also occur in neglected children or in poverty situations where feeding is likely to be more associated to availability of food.
4. Reluctant nursing. If the mother is tense during the nursing experience, the flow of milk is likely to be unsatisfactory and frustrating for the infant.
5. Agitated feeding. If the nurturing person is not comfortable during the feeding, the discomfort is likely to be transferred to the child.
6. Nonstroking during feeding. Mechanical feeding is experienced by the infant as unnatural and ungratifying.

Symbiosis

The normal mother experiences her dependency on the symbiosis as at a peak during the latter stage of the pregnancy, and from that time on it is experienced by her as a gradually decreasing state of dependency. During the first few weeks and months of the baby's life, especially if the child is breast nursing, the symbiosis is experienced at a high level by the mother and not at all by the infant, who is unaware of anything external. Between one and two months of age the child begins to experience the symbiosis as a specific attachment to a nurturing person, usually the mother, and from that time through the next two to three years extended separation of the child from the nurturing individual is inadvisable.

Mid-infancy

From the approximate age of six months until past the beginning of the second year, children are entering a new stage of independence. They become mobile, develop control over their body, and discover a great deal about how it works and what it will do (and not do). Teething and biting are important. They are another bridge between the internal and external and involve that all-important organ, the mouth. Smiling and babbling are important too; speech forms into meaningful patterns both as heard and as attempted.

A tremendous amount of learning takes place in relation to the external environment as children begin to explore. Motivation, awareness of internal experiences and interaction with the environment on the basis of those internal stimuli, are of major importance. Also, many perceptual tasks are accomplished at this time, and the fantasy structure which will later be necessary to thinking, memory, and organization, is initiated (Little Professor).

Symbiosis

The symbiosis is experienced as most significant for infants at approximately eight months of age. At that time they are aware of their dependency. Their mother's proclivity for going away is experienced as incredible, inexplicable loss, producing their first experience with grief. The frustration of this state of affairs motivates the child in the direction of becoming independent so that the threat of separation (abandonment or rejection) at later ages is experienced at a level of frustration that is tolerable for the child (not life-threatening). Increased self-definition, weaning, exploratory activity, and self-feeding are healthy characteristics of this stage for the child for whom the symbiosis is proceeding in a satisfactory manner.

For the parents, this period is likely to be frustrating. Children, as they teeth, drool, smear, and become increasingly mobile are less appealing to the nurturing parts of the Child parents. The care of a child during this period is likely to be Parent-programmed, with a decrease in efficiency and investment. If not experienced at an excessive level, this can be productive for both the parent and the infant in terms of growing autonomy which is mutually satisfactory. However, guilt may be produced in the parent as a result of unresponsiveness to the child, and this may result in increased discounting and noninvolvement. The child may learn to whine or escalate to elicit guilty nurturing as a form of stroking, or may become passive and overadapted.

Later Infancy

After children have established their autonomy in such areas as locomotion and self-feeding, when the distress of teething has begun to wane, and when they manage to be more or less free of such artificial restraints as play pens and cribs, a new period emerges. Previously the children have established that they exist and can do things. At this time (beginning at 12 to 15 months of age) they begin to find out what *other* things do. Curiosity emerges as a driving force, and children are hopeful, if not convinced, that when they complete their exploration of the universe they will have control over all things. The rapid learning which naturally happens at this time reinforces that expectation. On a day-to-day basis children are learning so much in a world still sufficiently small, that should that rate of learning continue in a nonexpanding environment, it might be reasonable to assume that they would become king of all they surveyed.

The toddlers are busily investigating such problems as, where do things go when I cannot see them? How frequently can I elicit smiles in response to my smile? They like the world to be in order and will compulsively close drawers and cupboards. When things don't work as they are supposed to, the toddlers often respond with indignation rather than fright. Animate and inanimate objects are not differentiated, and when they have negative experiences with their environment, they experience grief and frustration as though the slight were intentional. They are beginning to discover, but do not yet understand, that some of the more frustrating encounters are indeed intentional on the part of nurturing persons in the environment (who sometimes are not experienced as so very nurturing). The toddlers assume, however, that when they have accomplished all the learning they feel compelled to undertake, and which is paying off so reliably, they will have that phenomenon under control.

The issue is control, and the basic position is naively optimistic. With healthy parenting the external environment offers unconditional support and strokes, and the child is appealing, spontaneous, and responsive.

Symbiosis

As the more difficult middle infancy stage fades into the past, the infant becomes increasingly socially responsive, and parenting can begin to be verbal, requiring less energy output in the care of the infant. The parents are likely to again feel positive and nurturing towards the infant. Thus a pattern is begun which is likely to occur throughout childhood, of a good (gratifying) stage following a more difficult stage. The difficult stages are significant in promoting the breakdown of the symbiosis for both the parents and the infant, and the more gratifying stages serve the function of maintaining the ongoing investment in the relationship and reinforcing the infant's investment in positive strokes as a resource.

The Terrible Twos

As their awareness of the external environment matures, babies begin to suspect a dreadful possibility. For a long time they have operated as though all that is external to them will eventually come under their control. However, as they grow, their environment is enlarging also, and as they solve problems, new problems keep presenting themselves. It begins to be apparent that things are not proceeding as expected.

Most difficult to understand and control are people. Infants are compelled to interact with them because of their continued dependency, but these outsiders' penchant for interfering with the gratification of the infants is not being successfully resolved. One day the answer dawns. They are no longer able to avoid the distressing awareness that the world does not revolve around them; that other people are separate and have feelings and wants, just as they do.

They respond with anger. Some of the anger may be biological, but much of it is outrage and frustration over the discovery of the demand that they give up some of the autonomy they were anticipating. They are depressed. They sulk and have temper outbursts. They provoke over and over again, assuring themselves of the truth of the situation. And as a result of their provocation, there is an escalation of external demands for recognition. The parents decide that since this misbehaving is obviously deliberate, the baby is old enough to begin to learn to behave, and the parents start to make demands for adaptive behavior. Children respond to these demands with increased outrage, keeping themselves in an ongoing state of discomfort.

Obviously this state of affairs cannot continue indefinitely; it is too uncomfortable for both the child and the parents. If the relationship is healthy, and the child has awareness of the parents as a necessary source of strokes and nurturing, and if the parents are reasonable, consistent, and determined in their demands, the child will give in and adapt to them. As a result of this adaptation, the youngster makes a social contract. The child will relinquish autonomy for certain external rewards and will learn to share the world with all of the rest of the people who also have rights.

A whole new vista of learning opens up. No longer will spontaneous reactions to external stimuli be workable; in many instances children must negotiate to determine how they can get what they want without infringing more than necessary on what others want. They must learn what to do with feelings, and some of this learning will come from experimentation. They will try out different feelings, their expression, and productivity, to find out what the responses will be. They will also watch what others do and imitate them. They will have to learn to differentiate feelings into categories of appropriate and inappropriate, according to whether they can hope for a positive response to their expressions. Otherwise they will be left with feelings for which there is no behavioral outlet.

Script issues include decisions as to how much the youngsters will give, what they expect to get, and how much they will have to think in order to do that. A resolution to this stage precipitates the cathexis of the Adult as an autonomous ego state, separate from A_1. The necessity of remembering in order to meet all of the new expectations is a major source of motivation, and some children, where there is not a successful resolution, do not begin to utilize their full Adults at this time.

Symbiosis

It is important that the parents permit themselves a full range of affect in their relationship to the child, utilizing their feelings to help the youngster experience the necessity of social conformity, while still offering the protection of their caring and nurturing. Many unhealthy resolutions to this stage, in which the parents permit or encourage the child to act out their own rebelliousness, or are reluctant to make demands, result in games and thinking disorders. The too early communication of expectations is another likely mistake, resulting in overadaptation and incomplete experiencing of the conflict at this time.

The Trusting Threes

The sullen, demanding two-year-old emerges into a delightful, seemingly spontaneous youngster who is clearly no longer an infant. The miniature person is vociferously incorporating culture. Bits of information, such as that boys grow up to be men, policemen put people into jail, and trucks may not be able to see little girls, are engulfed. This is the last year of the uniquely rapid learning that is characteristic of the Little Professor, and is utilized to enhance the new social adaptations by providing the child with a view of the culture. At the same time there is much observation and incorporation of social ritual.

Symbiosis

This is an easy stage, characterized by mutual stroking and closeness in families where affection is easily expressed. Touching continues to be important to the child, and is probably gratifying to the parents. The strokes exchanged and time spent in teaching and explaining are also important.

The Fearful Fours

The youngsters are growing up. Constant supervision and protective feedback are no longer reliably available. The children encounter problems which they must face independently. They recognize the world as a huge place presenting many conflicting demands and paradoxes; their definitions of reality are still fluid; they have difficulty differentiating memory, fantasy, and dreams; and there is considerable reinforcement for their confusion about how things work. They are probably given odd bits of misinformation, such as they can't stand asparagus; Santa Claus brings presents only to good children, and then they get presents (no matter how much they misbehave); and virtue is usually rewarded.

Internally the children still experience considerable drive to learn to control their environment, but they are becoming increasingly aware of the need to control themselves in relation to the environment and produce those adaptive behaviors which will result in problem-solving and strokes. Their ambition exceeds their success. Then they discover a new mechanism for forcing adaptation. Utilizing a combination of fantasy and the feeling of fear, children learn to create fantasies to scare themselves into conformity. Furthermore, the fantasies can be used to provide punishment when external parenting is insufficient. We call this mechanism Witch Parent, and its function is to provide internal controls when the child experiences external controls as inadequate in relation to environment stress or threat. Thus, children who are not getting sufficient firm parenting in areas where welfare and safety are issues are most likely to experience difficulties with this stage (nightmares and excessive fears), and children who experience a secure external structure will have less difficulty. However, most children do experiment with the utilization of fear as a form of motivation and also of gratification (especially since it is likely to be associated with stroking).

Symbiosis

The parents are likely to experience ambivalence regarding the urgency with which the child demands protection and reassurance concerning fantasies and fears which have been created inside the child's head. There are impulses to provide comfort and reassurance and other impulses to express irritation at the irrationality of the demands. Probably both of these reactions are helpful to the child, and either one alone would be destructive. Making sure that children have the internal resources with which to deal with social demands (that they have acquired the habit training and can meet external expectations appropriate to their age) is important. Children should be encouraged to begin to provide solutions to their own problems.

Example: "I don't believe there is a tiger under you bed. If you think that, then I think you are making it up, and you can figure out what to do about it."

Five- to Eight-year-olds

The first autonomous step is taken into the larger world, as children start school. Nursery school may have offered some preparation for dealing with the group process, but the protected environment of a nursery school is quite different from the early experiences of being on one's own. Children now have to compete for strokes and attention from grown-ups and peers with diverse backgrounds and views, and to necessarily rely on the self to solve problems. They have incorporated a great deal of extraneous Parent, which they now find to be useless; for the first time they are aware that their Parent and others' may be different, and recognize that incorporating structure is not going to solve all problems. They are vulnerable to external criticism or teasing, and their feelings stick out like a sore thumb. In many situations they won't know how to protect themselves from being hurt. As a matter of fact, for many children, there may not be permission to do that, in that the children have been supposed to be vulnerable to criticism from people outside themselves (parents and playmates).

Symbiosis

Parents often experience some relief at the growing independence of their children, that they are less demanding of time and attention. It is likely that for the first time the problems of the children will not actively involve the parents, although the parents are likely to be aware that the problems are occurring. What the children need from the parents is reassurance that they can independently explore ways of dealing with the problems, and permission to protect themselves from being hurt by being aware of reasons and being less vulnerable.

Example: "You don't have to take seriously everything people say. Sometimes people say things just to get attention or to sound important." The child may also need permission to examine and perhaps violate previous parental injunctions; i.e., "I would not like you to be the kind of person who chooses to deal with issues by hitting, but situations may come up where you decide to hit because that seems the best thing to do at the time. Since I can't always be around to decide those things for you, you'll have to figure them out for yourself."

Eight- to Twelve-year-olds

This period is activity oriented. Children defend against feelings in the service of other functions. Parent values are compared among groups of children (i.e., "Other kids don't have to work for their allowances"), and there is some considerable altering of the Parent ego state. Parenting is typically sought from others in the community, (teachers, scoutmasters, clergymen, the parents of friends). Children are acquiring new options for relating and testing limits. Aggression and competition are rampant, and escalated encounters with peers and authorities are sometimes courted, as the children are developing internal defense mechanisms for the protection of their Child. Skills are important and a lot of scripting about doing things comes from this stage.

The Parent ego state is cathectable as an autonomous ego state toward the end of this period, and for much of the time children are very script conscious.

Symbiosis

Parents are likely to find this period aggravating. It will seem as though the child is actively defending against or challenging parental values much of the time, and to a large extent this is true. However, the function of doing that has less to do with the particular values involved and is more relevant to the internal resources the child is developing with which to encounter problems in the future. It is important for parents to stay involved, be expressive of their feelings, and make ongoing demands for conformity. Toward the end of this period, after the Parent ego state is fully cathectable, the child should be encouraged to consider problems in social interaction not simply in terms of consequences, or cause and effect, but from a value orientation.

Example: "I'd suggest you think about the argument with Johnny from the position of what kind of friend you are and what kind of person or friend you want to be."

Adolescence

Adolescence has as its developmental goal that the children should be, at the termination of this period, capable of physical autonomy. They should be able to sustain themselves in the culture both economically and socially, and have resources for obtaining gratification.

Earlier in this stage the youngsters are likely to reexperience conflict left over from developmental tasks unresolved from younger stages. Physical changes and changes in self-image are likely sources of conflicts and confusion. Issues of adequacy are encountered initially from a position of little confidence. Children hope for the best and fear the worst; they are busy with the task of defining a place for themselves in the grown-up world. Values are an important issue, and by mid-adolescence the individual should be functioning primarily from a value structure rather than a rule structure. This is likely to involve some testing, having as its aim forcing either more parenting from external authority figures in areas where values are not functional, or forcing issues of self-assertion, (decisions about the kind of person the individual will become).

There is a deepening of potential for intimacy. Children experience a reawakening of their feelings, and are once again vulnerable to external definition, but with the added resources for self-protection that they have acquired during the previous developmental stage. Closeness emerges into a concern about sex, and the adolescents begin sexual experimentation. Confusions and problems are likely to be acted out at an escalated level, perhaps because of the urgency of impending maturity.

Symbiosis

Parents must be reactive to the individual child. Depending on the child's previous involvement in family interactions, some children may need more intimacy and stroking and involvement during this period than others. Many children need to find their own way and make their own mistakes. Parents should, of course, make sure those mistakes are not disastrous for the child's future, but unless previously neglected, authority should be used infrequently during this period. Rather, children should experience growing awareness of their parents as people separate from themselves, and their problems and needs, and experience the parental demands as part of the demands of the external environment, the demands perhaps having special emphasis (or de-emphasis) according to the needs of the children and the quality of the relationship the children have with their parents. Parents' reaction to this stage vary. Some parents are reluctant to experience the separation; others are glad to have successfully discharged their responsibility, and are eager to see the children as independent. Whatever the parents' and children's reactions are to one another, it is important that the children enter the period of establishing independence from a position of knowing that their parents expect them to be successful in solving problems.

Young Adulthood

The period immediately following physical separation, generally the young adult period, is difficult for many individuals, especially in our mobile culture where the separation is likely to be over a considerable distance. Major issues at this time are establishing an independent stroking economy, accomplishing economic autonomy, and utilizing cultural values in preference to parental values. The latter has been of particular concern for many individuals in recent years because of rapid changes in cultural values around such areas as social roles, sexual behavior, drug use, marital and parenting responsibilities, and economic values.

Symbiosis

Most difficult for many parents is adapting to the values adopted by their children as a result of social change. Parents and children need to arrive at a contract which permits each to have autonomous values and which structures a relationship based on mutual respect. Frequently parents stubbornly refuse to accept different values in their children; however, with equal frequency parents attempt to adapt to life styles which are not acceptable to their value systems by discounting the discomfort. The most healthy relationships occur when there can be frank discussion of differences, and when compromises can be found which are mutually acceptable.

Fixations

When developmental tasks are not accomplished successfully, the individual has difficulty proceeding to subsequent developmental stages. Following adolescence, there will be marked indications pointing out those stages where a great deal of Child energy is still bound up. A complete diagnostic guide cannot be provided in the space available here, but a few highlights might be helpful to the reader in understanding how a regressive technique could be useful to assist the patient in breaking through fixations by experiencing new external parental involvements.

Individuals who have problems pre-dating two years of age are likely to demonstrate considerable oral behavior, agitation, and poor quality of thinking. They may be very suggestable and adaptable, and use denial as a defense mechanism if the problem originates in early or late infancy. Mid-infancy disturbances are more likely characterized by hassling and projecting. The mouth is identified as the most sensitive part of the body, and there are likely to be impulses to suck or bite. Feelings are not reliably discriminated from one another.

The two-year-old stage is characterized by negativism, such as, "I won't," "I can't," or "I don't want to," position, and the justification (grandiosity) is "I don't care!" The invitation is "Try and make me!"

Problems originating in the three- to eight-year-old stage are likely to be demonstrated as oversensitivity, fearfulness, manipulations, and social naivete. Eight- to twelve-year-old issues are also negativistic, often passive-aggressive, but distinct from two-year-old negativism in that the issues are less primitive and more task oriented.

Example: The child rarely finishing things. Generally at this age the issues are script issues and can be identified with specific parental injunctions.

Adolescent issues are related to shallowness, lack of value orientation, and self-definition. These individuals have difficulty identifying a place for themselves in society, and may be identified with sub-groupings of dubiously functional individuals.

All of these disturbances may be compensated in a myriad of ways, but in a treatment structure where there is protection and permission for people to do what they need to do, the issues are likely to emerge fairly readily. One precaution: sometimes individuals maintain cathexis to the developmental stage immediately prior to that stage wherein the problem would be encountered as a means of insuring ongoing comfort and maximum functioning. In that case a regressive technique would not be useful in exploring the ego state which is most readily cathectable, and this is not a true fixation. Generally patients are aware of what they are doing and why they are doing it, and, again, if the treatment structure offers a resolution to the problem, they are likely to take advantage of it, although their involvement may initially be cautious and confusing to the therapist.

Chapter Five

FRAME OF REFERENCE AND REDEFINING

A large proportion of the treatment at Cathexis Institute has consisted of working towards major reorganization of personality structure and equally major rescripting. The concepts developed for understanding the passivity syndrome (See Chapter Two), developmental theory and information (See Chapter Four), information on the structure and dynamics of the different pathologies (See Chapter Six), and general TA personality and communication theory, provide a myriad of specifics to use in this treatment. However, when working for major change, a broader perspective which includes and integrates these specifics is often useful. The concepts of "frame of reference" and "redefining" give two such perspectives and additionally provide specific references to the patient's perceptions.

FRAME OF REFERENCE

Each of a person's ego states has its own structural and functional characteristics whose origins can be clearly identified. (See Chapter Three). Moreover, the Parent, Adult, and Child ego states are connected structurally and integrated functionally into a whole which is characteristic of the overall person. Frame of reference refers to this overall structural and functional matrix.

Definition

An individual's frame of reference is the structure of associated (conditioned) responses (neutral pathways) which integrates the various ego states in response to specific stimuli.

Structure and Function

It provides the individual with an overall perceptual, conceptual, affective, and action set, which is used to define the self, other people, and the world, both structurally and dynamically. In particular, it is the framework within which the individual answers such questions as: "How do I know I exist?" and "Who am I?" It can be thought of as the skin that surrounds the ego states binding them together and acting as a "filter" on reality. (See Fig. 8.)

Script options are defined by the frame of reference which is initially learned from the parents and determines the structure of thinking, problem-solving, and other adaptive behaviors.

Frame of reference is both transactional and psychodynamic (See Fig. 9). The vectors between each individual's ego states represent path-

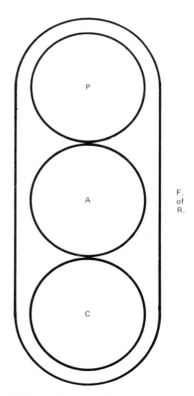

FIG. 8. Frame of Reference

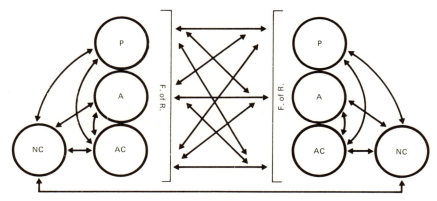

FIG. 9. Structure and Dynamics of Frame of Reference

ways of cathexis (energy shifts). The vectors between the individuals represent transactions. Each stimulus or response is conceived from the initiator's frame of reference and perceived from the listener's frame of reference. Natural Child to Natural Child transactions between people occur when a frame of reference is shared or dropped. This appears to be most likely to occur in nonverbal transactions, and we would see intimacy as involving some such transaction and fights for survival as involving others.

The personality is structured with the Natural Child as the source of motivation, and with the Parent, Adult, and Adapted Child all functioning as adaptive structures within the framework of reality definitions which have been learned out of social experience. (See Chapters Three and Four).

Intervention

Changes in the frame of reference result from (1) the Child becoming uncomfortable with the present frame of reference and seeking Adult information and new permission, (2) the Child becoming uncomfortable with the present frame of reference and seeking new permissions, or (3) a Parent (external) structure "imposing" a new frame of reference. In all cases, frame of reference change is only complete when the new definitions are integrated into all three ego states as Parent-OK, Adult-factual, and Child-problem-solving.

Reparenting involves a massive reorganization of frame of reference (See Chapter Seven). However, less complex change can be accomplished for those patients with whom contamination is not a major complication by aligning the Adult and Child in a redecision. This intervention involves the adaptation to new information provided externally, which must then be consistently practiced in order to establish new associational patterns.[10] The patient will then actively seek new Parent to confirm the redecision.

The role of the Parent in a person's frame of reference is of pivotal significance. Its significance arises from the influence of the parents or other nurturing individuals on early childhood definitions. The definitive function of the Parent is at least as significant as its nurturing and critical functions. It is, moreover, especially relevant to frame of reference, since Parental definitions lay down the parameters for all a person's thinking, feeling, and behavior. For example, the Parent defines how the Child might get strokes; the meaning of OKness and not-OKness, and how each applies to the Child; and the meaning of words such as "good," "bad," "nice," "hard," "want," and "need."

In treatment some situations determining the patient's frame of reference and undertaking systematic change by selectively redefining or eliminating referential words (*examples:* "OK," "adequate," "want") can in itself effect major changes in thinking and behavior.

Example: A patient expressed fear of being inadequate in a job. She was told to stop using any internal measure of "adequate" and instead to define specific goals and relate only to clearly stipulated, externally-defined criteria (e.g., production quotas). Anxiety was reduced and efficiency increased.

To be meaningful, transactions between people require agreement on a frame of reference, or at least a belief that there is agreement. For example, people discussing whether a third person is OK, both accept as a frame of reference that some people are not-OK. However, unless they determine what each of them means by OK, miscommunication may occur through each person assuming that the other person is utilizing the same frame of reference.

---

10. Goulding, R., "New Directions in Transactional Analysis," *Progress in Group and Family Therapy,* ed. C. J. Sager and H. S. Kaplan (New York: Brunner/Mazel, 1972), Chapter 9.

In analyzing games, it is valuable to determine the adaptive positions in the games. The initial move in a game can be established by the player in any position (Victim, Persecutor, or Rescuer),[11] and the game is confirmed (the second discount) when the other players adapt to the frame of reference presented by the initiator.

Example: Persecution: "You're not-OK because ..."
Victim: "I'm sorry ..."
Rescuer: (to persecutor) "You should be more understanding",
(to Victim) "Shouldn't he?"

In this example the Persecutor defines some people as not-OK, the Victim confirms this assumption, and the Rescuer also confirms the assumption but uses Parent in an attempt to redefine the situation.

Clinically it is useful to determine the nature of the frame of reference and identify the adaptive positions (who is adapting to whose frame of reference). The next step is to get the people to define verbally their own frame of reference. This procedure cathects the Adult, breaks down the symbiosis (See Chapter Two) and also provides an opportunity to check out whether there is misinformation. It is also a means of confronting games in a nonthreatening manner and is productive in teaching people to confront games in a social context (e.g., "What does the word 'violence' mean to you?").

There are characteristic frames of reference associated with certain diagnoses. They are characteristic because characteristic injunctions and decisions are predetermining factors in the development of pathology, which also influences the likely structure of contaminations and exclusions. Familiarity with the frame of reference associated with a specific pathology provides a structured point of intervention. (See Chapter Seven).

One of the interesting considerations regarding the significance of frame of reference is that individuals with nonconventional frames of reference seem to have options which are not available to most people in our society. In working with people diagnosed schizophrenic, for example, we have seen instances of nonacceptance of pain, control of the autonomic nervous system, the intentional production of internal

---

11. Karpman, "Fairy Tales and Script Drama Analysis."

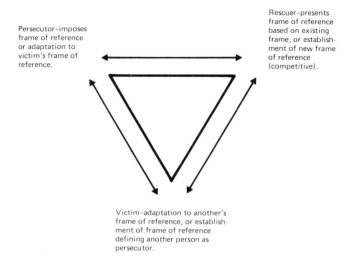

FIG. 10. Frame of Reference and Game Positions

injuries, and remarkable instances of healing. Such phenomena as the miraculous production of stigmata or the capacity to walk over fire (both well documented occurrences) seem relevant.

The ability of therapists (teachers, clergymen, scoutmasters) to redefine frame of reference depends on the potency their Parent, Adult, and Child ego states are perceived to have by the person's Child. In many situations this depends on the potency with which they are utilized. In effective treatment, redefinition is Adult-programmed and is not undertaken until there is as great an understanding (as possible) of the patient's frame of reference and how it is detrimental to the patient's welfare. Therapists need to be cognizant of their own frame of reference and also aware that there are many frames of reference which are functional. The whole question, "What is really real?" is necessarily an ongoing consideration.

REDEFINING

Definition

Redefining refers to the mechanism people use to maintain an established view of themselves, other people, and the world (frame of reference) in order to advance their scripts. It is the internal mechanism people use to defend themselves against stimuli which are inconsistent with their frames of reference and redefine the stimuli to fit in. Its three components are discounting, grandiosity, and thinking disorders (See Chapter Two).

Several generalizations have emerged from the work so far. Firstly, on the one hand, it appears that whenever people redefine, their behavior is gamey or scripty; and, on the other hand, when people are not redefining but are acting and reacting to stimuli as they are in reality, they may be behaving autonomously. Secondly, redefining is used with the four passive behaviors to confirm or enforce the type of symbiotic relationships people require to advance their scripts. Thirdly, when people redefine, their options are limited by the structure of the symbiotic relationships their redefining and behavior establishes; when not redefining, people can determine and act on their own options without these restrictions.

In therapy there are many obvious redefinitions. Therapy itself is a threat to a person's frame of reference and under this threat people tend to externalize much of the thinking they would otherwise keep to themselves. It appears that the more confrontive the therapy, the more obvious redefinitions become. An example of an obvious redefinition is:

A: "You're playing a game with me."
B: "I'm not. I'm just sitting here trying to talk to you. You're playing the game."

With minimal recognition of the issue A raises, B redefines the issue, firstly, to talking, and secondly to A being the game player. If B is successful, the redefinition will divert the threat to A who is likely to start defending rather than keeping to the original issue. However, there are many other less obvious examples. Redefining is most obvious when people's frames of reference are inconsistent and threatened. On the other hand, when there is agreement in the frames of reference of two people, their redefinitions may go unchallenged.

Therapeutically the problem is to confront the process in such a way that the people become aware of what they are doing and develop an investment in not doing it. We have found that a five-fold focus used simultaneously in treatment seems to get the best results. We focus on the symbiotic basis of redefining, which isolates three distinctive redefining relationships: the internal components of the mechanism, the transactional aspects of redefining, the behavioral aspects, and we focus on six different roles adopted when people redefine.

Symbiotic Basis

Originally people depend on getting what they need within symbiotic relationships with their mothers and other significant caretaking people. When all goes well this symbiosis is broken down as children learn to think independently and take responsibility for their own perceptions, thoughts, feelings, and behaviors. They become autonomous individuals. Wherever this autonomy is undercut by parental scripting and consequent decisions by the Child, some aspects of the symbiosis remain intact in an unhealthy, option limiting form.

Originally a baby needs the symbiosis to survive, and survival remains equated to some degree with any unresolved aspects of the symbiosis. To meet the needs which are connected with the remnants of the symbiosis, people continue to act in later life towards others as they did in the original relationships. They are aware of no other options for themselves. Therefore, they actively seek out people who will relate to them in the same way and attempt to get those who would not do so spontaneously to do so anyway.

Even in later life the stakes are the same. A threat to later symbiotic relationships is experienced as a threat to survival (getting needs met) at the same level as it was perceived to be threatened when the person was a child. The person's reaction depends on the degree of threat experienced when a relevant injunction was accepted in childhood. Thus, for example, thinking in the face of a "Don't think" injunction may involve anything from mild discomfort to an extinction anxiety.

However, the reality is that grown people can get their needs met best by relating autonomously and not within unhealthy symbiotic relationships. Any other perception (actual or implicit) is a redefinition of reality.

Symbiosis, therefore, is the cause and effect of redefining, while survival, or getting needs met, is the goal and motivation. To some extent this explains the experience of redefining people report. It is an experience of insecurity or inadequacy in the present, which is directly related both to an unresolved past and a hoped for but uncertain future.

Internal Mechanism

We need to filter and structure stimuli (internal and external) in order to understand them in ways which enable us to get what we need. As we grow we learn which stimuli are significant, what their significance is, and how to structure related stimuli into gestalts upon which we can act effectively. When this learning leads us to ignore certain simuli, distort their significance, or put them together in gestalts which distort reality so that we are symbiotically dependent or limiting our options unrealistically, then we are redefining.

The three components of the mechanism are discounting, grandiosity, and thinking disorders. All operate simultaneously to produce a redefined view of ourselves, other people, and the world. The appearance of any of them is a sign that redefining is occurring, and each may usefully become the focus of treatment (See Chapter Two).

The type and mode of discounting indicates the degree of pathology in the redefinition. The amount of distortion produced by the grandiosity is related to the degree of threat the person experiences in response to the stimulus of the redefinition; that is, the threat to the symbiosis. The thinking disorders are related to problems and option definitions and, therefore, to the person's action possibilities.

Example: Susie, a hebephrenic girl, asked for something to eat. She was told to wait for five minutes until the food was ready. She immediately got violent. After the incident she reported "I thought you wanted to kill me" (Grandiosity). "You said I couldn't eat." (Discounting that she was told to "wait"—most pathological because it was a discount of stimuli at the highest level.) "Now I remember you've asked me to wait before and fed me when you said you would. I didn't think of that." (Overdetailing on the one incident without attention to her more general experience.) Being asked to wait was redefined into a potentially homicidal response.

Redefining Transactions

We have found that people with conflicting or inconsistent frames of reference use two distinctive types of transactions when they redefine.

Whenever these transactions occur someone is redefining. They are *tangential* and *blocking* transactions. They may be used from any ego state, although if used by the Adult without awareness, the person is in a contamination. In both types of transactions the focus of the stimulus is different from the focus of the response. The respondent discounts some aspect of the stimulus and shifts the issue. The more subtle the shift, the less it is likely to be detected. In addition, since these transactions are usually complementary, they often appear to be straight.

Tangential Transactions

Tangential transactions are transactions in which the stimulus and response address different issues or address the same issue from different perspectives.

If allowed to run their full course, conversations involving these transactions are characterized by a constant shifting of focus away from the issue being discussed, especially the original issue. The participants appear to "talk past" each other and not "to" each other. These conversations can move in circles several times with one or both parties confusedly realizing from time to time, "I've been this way before" or "This is getting nowhere." The issue remains unaddressed in the middle of all the perspectives and other issues. Significantly, no one confronts the shifts effectively, and most of the people involved are likely to have "forgotten" the original issue.

Examples:
1. A: Who did that?
   B: It happened before dinner.
      (Shift from "who" to "when")
2. A: Will you do it?
   B: I'll be able to (one day perhaps).
      (Shift from "intention" to "potential")
3. A: What are you going to do about it?
   B: I've already tried doing X.
      (Shift from "future" to "past")
4. A: You wash the car.
   B: I want to do the dishes.
      (Shift from "car" to "dishes")

A skillful person can prolong discussions using these transactions for long periods.

Blocking Transactions

Blocking transactions are transactions in which the purpose of raising an issue is avoided by disagreeing about the definition of the issue. They are frequently the first move in a chain of redefining transactions and are usually competitive. They are often used in a context where there is an accepted definition of the issue. The parties discount this, and the conversation gets bogged down in over-detailed and overgeneralized points of definition instead of dealing with the issue.

Example:
1. A: Stop agitating and think.
   B: I wasn't. I was only keeping time to the tune in my head.
      (Definition of "agitation")
2. A: Are you doing something? (being active?)
   B: Yes, I'm thinking.
      (Definition of "doing something")

We noted that these transactions may involve any of the ego states. When they occur without being confronted, all those involved are discounting. This means they are operating with Parent or Child exclusions or from contaminations. They discuss things with each other "convinced" of their view. With each transaction the discounting escalates, and they will begin to experience discomfort without being aware of its origins. The discomfort is the price people pay for redefining. Their needs do not get met adequately.

When redefining from a Parent contamination, the Parent drains energy from the person's Adult whose perceptions and reactions are distorted by Parental prescriptions, definitions, assumptions, and values. From a Child contamination, the person's Adult perceptions are distorted by filtering them through Child decisions about feelings, wants and needs, decisions which are more relevant to the past than the present. When excluding Parent or Child, the person's Adult is not being used.

There are three levels to these transactions: a social level, a psychological level, and a symbiotic level. The basic symbiotic level messages are related to the players' preferred positions in the symbiosis (Child, or

Parent/Adult); the psychological level carries the ulterior messages related to the specifics of the symbiosis in the situation the people are in; and the social level contains the actual words being used.

To diagram these transactions clearly we have combined the normal transactional diagram of ulterior transactions with the structural diagram of symbiosis (See Chapter Two) and a variation of Ernst's approach to duplex transactions involving contaminations[12] (See Figures 11, 12, 13). The continuous boundaries around the ego states show each person's preferred position in the symbiosis with each other at a particular point in time. The dotted arrows refer to the psychological level messages specific to the situation, and the continuous arrows refer to the social level messages. (Where exclusions are involved, the social and psychological level messages coincide, and the Adult boundaries are dotted for the person with the exclusion).

Redefining Relationships

Our understanding of redefining transactions highlights three significant types of redefining relationships: symbiotic, Parent-competitive, and Child-competitive relationships. They are significant because the dynamics of each type are different, and the treatment procedures necessary for interrupting them successfully are different.

These relationships are more or less transitory. In an ongoing relationship between two people, that is, they are likely to move into all three ways of relating to each other at different times. When relating in a Child-competitive way, they will compete over who is going to get needs met or express feelings. In the Parent-competitive relationship, the competition is over who is going to define situations and take responsibility for the other. The aim of both types of competition is to reestablish the symbiotic relationship. In addition, while they will switch positions in the symbiosis from time to time, each person appears to have a general preference for one of them. The position they occupy at a particular moment will depend on the "symbiotic contract" in their overall relationship: the contract around getting Child needs met, dealing with feelings, thinking, and deciding who is respon-

---

12. Ernst, F. H. Jr., *Who's Listening,* Addresso' set (Vallejo, California, 1968), p. 7.

sible for these in particular situations. Where there is agreement, the symbiotic type of relationship is likely to be present. For example, "My husband handles the family's finances. I take care of the housework." Where there is disagreement the Child- or Parent-competitive types are likely to appear. For example, "We always fight over money" (Child-competitive); "We never agree on what's best for the children" (Parent-competitive).

The particular combinations of these three types of relationships that people adopt, the games they play within them, who they set them up with, where they set them up, when they do so, and their preferred positions in the symbiosis are determined by, firstly, the nature of the early symbioses they were involved in as a child and, secondly, their script decisions. With this interpretation, the furthering of peoples scripts and the games they play are seen as an ongoing sequence of symbiotic relationships, or competitive relationships established with the purpose of securing a symbiotic relationship.

Symbiotic Type

The transactional paradigm of this type of redefining relationship is shown in Figure 11. (Figures will not be given for symbioses involving exclusions.)

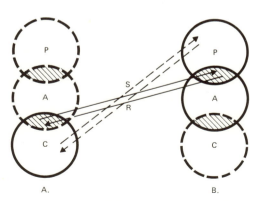

FIG. 11. *Transactional Paradigm of Redefining Relationship— Symbiotic Type*

In this type of relationship A and B generally expect B to take care of A, define situations and do the thinking. They also expect A to express feelings, make demands around needs, and take only token responsibility for perceptions, thinking, feeling, behaviors, and meeting of those needs. Child needs and feelings are discounted by B, and Parent and Adult abilities are discounted by A. Both collect stamps with each transaction involving these discounts. The stroke economy of the relationship may involve positive and/or negative strokes. On the Karpman Drama Triangle, A tends to be an actively provocative or passive Victim, while B tends to be a Rescuer or Persecutor.

A operates from a Child contamination (exclusion), and B operates from a Parent contamination (exclusion).

Social level:
 A: "X is the way things are here."
 B: "You're wrong. It's Y. (or Yes you're right. Well done.)"
Psychological level: (between Parent and Child)
 A: (C→P) "I can't think for myself (am not responsible for my feelings, actions, etc.) here. Do it for me." (Say it's OK.)
 B: (P→C) "You're right. I can see that's true here. I'll do it for you." (It's OK.)
Symbiotic level:
 A: In the Child position being "cared for" (usually as a victim) for "being" not-OK.
 B: In the Parent/Adult position "caring" for A (usually as a rescuer or persecutor) because "he is" not-OK.

It is this type of relationship, or an overt symbiosis that people attempt to reestablish, confirm, or enforce by redefining. A perceives this relationship structure as the only way to get needs met in the situation. Similarly, although discounting needs and feelings, B's Child usually erroneously perceives that needs will be met in this situation by attempting to meet A's needs.

Parent-Competitive Type

This type of redefining relationship is based on a competition for the Parent/Adult position in the symbiosis. (See Figure 12). The stakes of

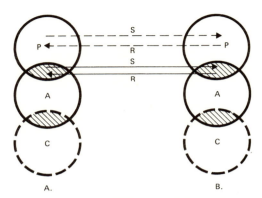

FIG. 12. *Transactional Paradigm of Redefining Relationship Parent-Competitive Type*

the competition are the "survival issue" because the symbiosis is threatened. Both people attempt to get the other to overadapt to their definition of the situation, issue, or event. Both are discounting feelings and needs, and are collecting stamps to justify the escalations they will use to establish the symbiosis with them in the Parent/Adult position. The strokes may be positive or negative, and the people may occupy any one of the three positions on the Karpman Drama Triangle. However, they usually attempt to occupy the same game position at the same time. Usually, there is a disagreement on frame of reference.

Both people operate from Parent contaminations (exclusions).

Social Level:
    A: "This is what is happening here."
    B: "I think you're wrong. It's like this."

Psychological Level:
    (usually P→P, sometimes crossed P→C, P→C)
    A: "X is how things should be here."
    B: "Y is how they should be."

Symbiotic Level:
    A: In the Parent/Adult position expecting B to let him "take care" of B for "being" not-OK so he can "take care" of himself.
    B: In Parent/Adult position expecting the same of A.

The competition ends for a time when A and B part company, or when one of them overadapts to the other and moves into a Child contamination (exclusion), so establishing a symbiosis. Because each has collected stamps, the stage is for further competitive encounters in the future. The more intensely the "survival issue" is experienced by both parties, the more escalated these encounters are likely to be. A's and B's encounters may range from a mildly irritated exchange to physical violence.

Child-Competitive Type

The competition in this type of redefining relationship is for the Child position in the symbiosis. (See Figure 13). Again the symboisis is threatened and the stakes revolve around the "survival issue." Each is demanding to be "taken care" of symbiotically and is discounting personal responsibility. They collect stamps with each transaction involving these discounts to justify the escalation they will use to force the issue. Strokes may be positive or negative. The favored positions on the Karpman Drama Triangle appear to be Victim and Persecutor, and both people usually attempt to occupy the same position simultaneously. The most intense competition tends to develop around the Victim position. Usually there is a disagreement on frame of reference.

Both A and B operate from Child contaminations (exclusions).

Social Level:
    A: "X is the way things are here."
    B: "It's not. It's like Y."
Psychological Level: (Usually C→C, sometimes crossed C→P, C→P)
    A: "I want things to be like X here. Or else! (Watch out!)"
    B: "I want them to be like Y. You watch out!"
Symbiotic Level:
    A: In Child position attempting to force B to "take care" of A for "being" not-OK.
    B: In Child position attempting to force the same from A.

The competition, when intense, quickly becomes a question of who is going to give way first to the Child escalations of the other. The competition stops, at least temporarily, when A and B part company, or when one of them shifts to the Parent/Adult position. "Losers" are likely to go in search of someone to take care of them symbiotically as

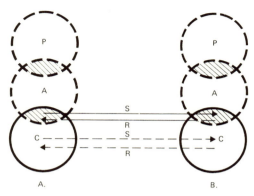

FIG. 13. Transactional Paradigm of Redefining Relationships Child-Competitive Type

quickly as possible. Of the three types of redefining relationships, this appears to be the most potentially explosive. The extent to which the parties are prepared to escalate is again determined by the degree of intensity with which they are experiencing their survival to be threatened within the symbiosis.

Redefining transactions occur in all three types of relationships. However, tangential and blocking transactions seem to be much more frequent in the two competitive types. This is because the symbiotic type involves complementary expectations. Both people agree on at least some of the redefinitions basic to the symbiosis. The competitive types involve conflicting expectations. The redefining is used to "resolve" the conflict by forcing the issue within the relationship, or by "forcing" a third party to intervene symbiotically.

Behaviors

All three of these relationships are characterized by shifts in responsibility, thinking, feeling, and discomfort. The shifts are achieved through the use of the four passive behaviors: doing nothing, overadaptation, agitation, and incapacitation or violence. Mounting agitation is one of the most reliable signs that redefining is taking place in situations where people appear to be putting equal energy into a discussion. The agitation may be verbal, bodily, or agitated thinking. However, each of the four behaviors, combined with the use of tangential and blocking transactions, may be used to achieve the shifts. As soon as a shift is made, a symbiosis has been established.

Redefining Roles

We see people's games and scripts as being acted out from six distinctive roles: *Caretaker, Hard Worker, Angry Righteous, Angry Wrongdoer, Woeful Righteous,* and *Woeful Wrongdoer.* These roles are adopted and shifted in the service of the script. The characteristics of each can be described in terms of related games.

While in one role, a person collects stamps in order to move to another when the script calls for it. The roles are related dynamically, and while people can move from one of them into any one of the other five, they seem to move through them in preferred orders. Some of the moves can be predicted by focusing on the two levels of game position associated with each role. There is an overt or social level position and a psychological level position in each role. The former refers to the game position occupied overtly. The latter refers either to a game position the people intend to occupy, or they are defending against, or one they are actually occupying at the psychological level but are hiding behind the overt position. (A person with good social control may act out the social level position at the psychological level, and the psychological level position at the symbiotic level.)

The possible shifts between the roles and their associated game positions are shown in the Redefining Hexagon in Figure 14. The letters over the slashes on the table refer to each role's social level position, and the letters under the slashes to the psychological level positions.

The favorite game of Hard Workers is often "Look How Hard I'm Trying." These people present themselves as putting a lot of energy into things. At the social level they are Rescuing. The group and the therapist (spouse, work associates) are supposedly not going to have to put much energy into helping them. However, the issues necessary to solve a problem will be studiously avoided. At the psychological level Hard Workers will be defending against, aiming at, or actually occupying the Victim or Persecutor positions. Hard Workers tend to operate out of a Child contamination or exclusion.

Caretakers usually play "I'm Only Trying to Help You." Their social level position is Rescuer, while their psychological level positions are Victim or Persecutor. They "take care" of others whether the others

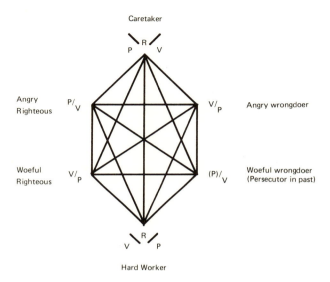

FIG. 14. *Redefining Hexagon Showing Redefining Roles and Positions*

ask for care or not and they tend to operate from a Parent contamination or exclusion.

Angry Righteous people present a social level position easily identifiable as Persecutor. They tend to play "Now I've Got You, You Son Of A Bitch" and usually come from a Parent contamination or operate with a Parent exclusion. At the psychological level the position they aim for, defend against, or occupy is Victim.

Woeful Righteous people are martyred and tend to play games like "Look What They're Doing To Me" and "Ain't it Awful." At the social level they are in Victim, while at the psychological level, the position is Persecutor. They tend to come from a Child contamination or exclusion.

Angry Wrongdoers present the Victim position at the social level but very clearly imply a potential or actual persecution at the psychological level. They tend to operate from a Child contamination or exclusion. Angry Wrongdoers tend to play a variation of "Kick Me," "Kick Me (If You Dare)," and look for opportunities for "Uproar."

Woeful Wrongdoers characteristically play "Poor Me," "Kick Me (Please!)," and "Don't Kick Me (Please?)." They are likely to have been

Persecutor at the social or psychological level before moving into this role. The social level may be Victim or appear straight, and the psychological level position is Victim. They almost always operate from a Child contamination or exclusion.

We have noted that relationships are competitive when two people attempt to relate symbiotically from the same position in the symbiosis, and that this type of competition may be intensified by simultaneous attempts to occupy the same game position. In terms of game position on the hexagon, noncompetitive relationships are formed along the six lines outlining the hexagon and along the lines making up the six-pointed star within it. Competitive relationships around game positions occur between Angry Wrongdoer and Woeful Righteous, at times between Angry Righteous and Woeful Wrongdoer, and between people attempting to occupy the same position on the hexagon in relation to each other. The relationship between Caretaker and Hard Worker may be competitive or noncompetitive. As can be seen from the figure, the social and psychological level positions in the roles allow for the development and flow of games and scripts within the structure of symbiotic relationships.

Treatment

When people redefine, it is a sure sign that something is happening which is a threat to their frames of reference. The key issue in treatment is to identify what is threatened. When this is identified people are in a position to do what is necessary to resolve the conflict between their view of reality and reality itself, and thereby give up their investment in the problem. During this work they may continue actively to redefine, as the work itself may maintain the threat.

In our work we focus on the five aspects of redefining discussed. Firstly, when an issue is raised or emerges as significant, any attempts to use tangential or blocking transactions to divert attention away from it are confronted. The therapist needs to be aware of the issues and withstand any attempts to redefine them by bringing the focus back to the issues if redefinition occurs. If another important issue emerges in the work, it needs to be specified as related to the first issue and discussed in relation to them.

Examples of this type of confrontation are:

"I think you're redefining. I'd like you to answer my question (stay with the original issue)."

"Yes I can see how that is important. I'd like to discuss that later after we finish with the first issue."

"That is not a response to what I said. Will you respond to what I said?"

Secondly, when making any intervention which confronts redefining, we have found that the ego states the therapist uses are extremely important. Apparently very similar interventions can have very different results. The important factor is that the therapist needs to avoid relating within an unhealthy symbiotic structure. If the therapist enters an unhealthy symbiosis with the person being confronted, the redefinition may be further confirmed.

In order to avoid establishing an unhealthy symbiosis the therapist must confront people acting in a Parent contamination or exclusion differently from people in a Child contamination or exclusion. The therapist needs to have all three ego states available and not act from contaminations or exclusions. Given this, effective confrontation then seems to depend on the emphasis given to each ego state. Optimal results seem to derive from: an Adult observation first, followed by an Adult report about the therapist's ego state which matches the contaminating or excluding ego state of the person, or finally the therapist directly cathecting that ego state.

Examples of such encounters would be:
1. *Patient:* (Child contamination, exclusion)
   Therapist: "I think you are doing—(Adult) and I am uncomfortable because—(Adult, report on Child)."
   or
   "I think you are doing—(Adult) and I am angry (scared, sad, happy) because—(Child)."
2. *Patient:* (Parent contamination, exclusion)
   Therapist: "I think you are doing—(Adult) and I think you should—(Adult report on Parent)."
   or
   "I think you are doing—(Adult) and you should (are to)—(Parent)."

The more strongly patients are cathected into Parent or Child, the more strongly the therapist needs to come from the same ego state. In effect what the therapist does is use the competitive characteristic of symbioses to stimulate the patients to shift ego states, think, and take responsibility for meeting their own needs in straight ways. Because symbiotic competitiveness may lead to escalations, the therapist may need to use the Parent ego state with people in Child and the Child ego state with people in Parent, but use them only as much as is required to contain escalations.

When the patients are thinking and taking responsibility for themselves, work can be done on the redefinitions, contaminations or exclusions; on shift of thinking, feelings, and responsibility; on the roles adopted; and on their investment in all of these. We have found that the results are best when the patients have information on all of these because it provides structure for thinking about the problem and its solutions.

Another guideline is useful. If either person has a statement to make it is important that it is put as a statement. If there is a question it should be asked directly. Setting these as ground rules helps to emphasize autonomy and individual responsibility for meeting needs. For example, a response to "I want to know what you are thinking" is likely to be symbiotic, whereas a response to "Will you tell me what you're thinking?" is not. It is useful, therefore, to confront any implied statements or questions and have them put directly.

Thirdly, when working on redefinitions, attention needs to be given to the discounting, grandiosity, and thinking disorders involved. Awareness of these helps people get in touch with the significant internal issues for them in the situation (See Chapter Two).

Fourthly, the passive behaviors are confronted directly (See Chapter Two), or by using a "selective rescue." We use the selective rescue in early encounters with people as a means of avoiding an escalation of any of the passive behaviors, while providing the people with a problem-solving structure which will help them cope with the situations they are in. This is not a Rescue in the classical sense because the therapist has Adult awareness of what is being done and of the likely consequences. When using this technique, it is essential that no one be made "not-OK" in the encounter. An example is people who are not thinking (e.g., playing "Stupid"), where it is obvious they could think if they decided to. The therapist says, "I would like to stop here and give you some time to think about X, and we will talk about it later." (X is the therapist's definition of what is to be though about.)

Lastly, we have found it very useful to teach the redefining roles. When doing this, having a copy of the Redefining Hexagon for people to refer to has been an asset. Identifying people in these roles often means redefinitions are identified which would have been missed otherwise, especially when people have compatible frames of reference. Sometimes a person's redefining role is more obvious than the redefinitions. Having identified the role, people's overt and covert game positions are clear and can be worked on. The nature of the psychological level position—that is, whether the position is the person's objective, is being defended against, or is being acted out—is especially relevant to the person's investment in adopting the role at that time. In addition, working on the role often opens a direct route to the script basis of what the person is doing.

Chapter Six

PATHOLOGY

Diagnosis

Diagnosis is important. It is used to define the therapeutic problem and enables us to relate information about successful interventions from one patient to another. It provides therapists with a frame of reference to make it possible for them to successfully communicate with the patient.

Example:
> *Patient:* It scares me when things eat houses.
> *Therapist:* There is nothing about eating you really need to be afraid of.
> *Patient:* But it might eat up the whole world. Then we would all disappear.
> *Therapist:* Eating and disappearing don't really go together, and you aren't at all likely to get eaten up. Very few people get eaten up by anything.
> *Patient:* Jonah got eaten up by the whale.
> *Therapist:* One example of something doesn't make it very likely. Anyway, even in the story, Jonah didn't disappear. If you stop putting together things that scare you and working yourself up, you could probably explain to me what you saw that did really scare you.
> *Patient:* Well, I saw this big machine that was eating up a house. It had a big mouth and was chomping on big boards.
> *Therapist:* Oh, you mean a bulldozer. That isn't a mouth. It's a machine that people use to tear down. . . .

The above dialogue occurred with a hebephrenic patient. Hebephrenics usually have delusions concerning eating. Given no previous contact with the patient, a therapist who is familiar with a hebephrenic frame of reference could start in the first few moments of contact to make meaningful interventions in relation to the misinformation and delusional structure. Moreover, the patient, excited and amazed at having finally found a therapist who "understands" and does not discount the patient's perceptions, is more likely to enter into a significant contract.

Diagnoses thus used are not just labels; consequently it is important that they not be loosely assigned. Patients are often referred with a whole string of different labels; we do not see diagnoses as changing. Personality structures are incorporated during early childhood, and while there may be layers of defenses, the basic mechanisms and thinking structures are consistent. Diagnoses commonly employed elsewhere are not ordinarily used by us since in our experience they don't describe any discrete categories. In addition, we work with patients whom we have not successfully diagnosed, rather than apply a label which may be incorrect. It is important that diagnoses and categorizing not be used rigidly, and that individual differences be recognized.

Competitive Frame of Reference

Pathological symbiosis inevitably sets up a competition. The issues are: How am I going to get what I want if there isn't enough to go around? or How am I going to get what I want if you won't give it to me? or What am I going to get out of it if I do?

For most people in our society a competitive frame of reference is unavoidable. Comparisons are so structured into our thinking that for many of us thinking becomes almost impossible without them. For some individuals, family culture exaggerates competition enormously, either in emphasizing similarities or in emphasizing differences. Most people compete from an expectation to lose; they learn to compete at a very early age when winning is improbable. Thus, they incorporate self-definitions which are contrary to success and winning. The parents who set up the competitive structure likewise see themselves as losing because of the conflict the whole problem engenders. Thus, everyone ends up in the Victim position, the game position which is most socially reinforced. Within such family structures, the parents and child then compete for Victim, each trying to define the other as Persecutor, each risking occasional excursions into Persecutor—thus, escalating the game—and then scurrying back into Victim in order to be OK. The Rescuer is in the "winning" position. Using Parent, the Rescuer is able to righteously define both the not-OK Persecutor and the pitiful Victim, thus perpetuating the game and assuring continued success.

The antithesis for competition is the setting of goals which are autonomously defined and realistic for individuals and their life situation. Goals which are Adult-screened provide a frame of reference in which success is possible, even probable, and OKness is not an issue.

OKness is in itself a competitive concept having no intrinsic usefulness. It is an externally incorporated concept used to manipulate the Child into social conformity and is generally unrelated to specific goals, such as strokes or achievements. OKness does not generally involve an internal value system which will provide structure for functioning, but rather it provides a structure for self-criticism, guilt, and suffering.

A treatment structure, to be effective, must deemphasize competitiveness; reassure people that they can get what they need themselves, not at someone else's expense; and break through the investment in Victim strokes. Agitation, which appears to have enormous significance to competitive structures, is a major focus of treatment.

Schizophrenia

Schizophrenia is characterized by a locked system of messages in the Parent, corresponding adaptations in the Child, and an Adult which is misinformed. Given an internally consistent frame of reference as dictated by the Parent and a Child adapted to it, the Adult does not acquire or use information which is inconsistent with the Parent. The adaptations are the result of reinforcement of adaptive response patterns around survival issues such as strokes and feeling, which are maladaptive to the society generally or the needs of the individual. With a Child who perceives the pathology as necessary for survival, a Parent who confirms this, and an Adult unable to contradict it, the person has no exit from the system without external intervention.

Nonpsychotics have mechanisms which permit them to adjust to discomfort in ways which relate to an external reality; the mechanisms may or may not be successful, but they deal with something external to the people. Psychotics have not experienced enough consistency between their frame of reference and the external world to develop those

Pathology 75

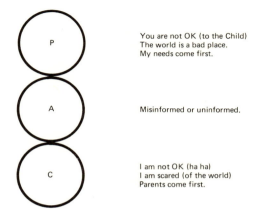

FIG. 15. *Basic Messages and Adaptations in Schizophrenia*

mechanisms. Therefore, in situations of discomfort or stress they are unable to find sufficient correlation between the two to enable them to continue to function in relation to the reality problem. They then retreat to a frame of reference which relates only to their internal experience or, at times when they are attempting to relate to the external reality, to an overadapted position, usually excluding their Child.

Connected Consciousnesses

It appears that integration of the activities of the hemispheres of the brain has considerable significance to schizophrenia. There may be relevant genetic factors, and there are certainly environmental factors. Lack of integration results in confused and distorted, but at times genuinely original and creative perceptions, in disruption and eruption in the fantasy mechanisms crucial to thinking, and in unusual utilizations of energy. One hemisphere may contain the internal perceptions of emotions which act as a focus for emotional energy generated. The other hemisphere may act as a receiver-transmitter where the generated emotional energy is analyzed and channelled into the environment with words being a major communication tool of latter-day humans. The discharge of this energy is related to survival, and if the energy is contained for a long enough period of time, the people emotionally implode. People can get to the point where there is an overwhelming internal blocking of the flow of energy if they have been externally reinforced in the nonexpression of feelings. Psychosis can be considered as an attempt to discharge the energy generated by both internal perceptions of emotions and conflicts resulting from unsuccessful attempts to change environmental stimulus.

This discharge and subsequent reorganization of self is a basic survival mechanism of humans, analogous to the molting of shells or skins seen throughout the animal kingdom (i.e., snakes, lobsters, butterflys, etc.). Drugs such as thorazine, prolixon, stelazine, mellaril, etc. (phenothiozines), prevent people from shedding their old "skin" and thus are ultimately self-destructive by not allowing individuals who enter a "psychosis" to complete this psychological, spiritual transformation. People who get such drugs are not allowed to find their natural self, Natural Child and are subjected to the uncomfortable side effects of such drugs which reinforce their not-OKness. These people face the risk of phenothiozine-created permanent brain damage called tardive dykinesia which has the symptoms of slow, distorted, uncontrollable muscle movements, especially around the mouth. There is evidence that failure to integrate the left and right hemispheres of the brain is relevant to the dichotomy and the polarization of the people's perceptions. This problem in communication may involve "learned blocks" between the left and right sides of the brain involving the corpus callosum. The corpus callosum is the large nerve network which connects the left and right cerebral hemispheres.

Regression can be viewed as an individual returning to the point in the maturation process where the blocks were created and attempting to work through the blocks in a new environment. Much of the work done in our programs involves techniques to facilitate this. Another technique which appears to involve a rehook-up of the hemispheres and a removal of the block are the hebephrenic resolutions which involve a violent discharge of giddiness and anger.

Hebephrenia

Hebephrenia is the most regressive of the schizophrenias and traditionally has the poorest prognosis. However, reparenting has proved effective with fifteen of these patients. There are many more hebephrenics than generally diagnosed, partly because of reluctance to use this diagnosis and partly because phenothiazenes selectively suppress giddiness as a symptom.

The personality is structured around a system of denial. This serves to keep the person fragmented so that certain needs and feelings which are not permitted, since they pose a threat to survival, can be kept out of awareness. The structure may be diagrammed to explicate the denial system (See Fig. 16).

There is prima facie evidence that failure to integrate the two hemispheres of the brain, involving "blockages" in the corpus callosum, is relevant to the dichotomy and the individual's perceptions of all issues as polarized.

Developmentally the child does not learn to identify the sensation of hunger because of early eating or nursing difficulties. Another important characteristic of the backgrounds of these patients is the excessive use of play pens or other artificial restraints (often until the ages of three to four years). This results in extreme over-adaptation with discounting and nonrecognition being the issue. The play pen situation means the mother can simply walk away and the child has no recourse. It also results in few normal internal controls being developed during this period, which leaves the patient with urgent problems of impulse control.

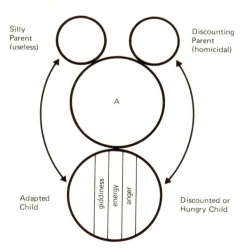

FIG. 16. *Hebephrenic Personality Structure*

Hunger is an ongoing issue; mouths are extremely important. Reality is defined competitively from internal referants. Passivity is alternated with frenetic outbursts of energy in the more active stages of the disturbance.

These patients are easily engaged in treatment because their extreme adaptability means they are appealing to therapists, and their extreme regressiveness results in ready responses to regressive techniques. Early in treatment dramatic improvement is characteristic. Then there are extended periods of running, rebelliousness, and conflict. Moreover, ongoing attention to the learning relevant to integrating the two parts of the brain and the eventual breakdown of the dichotomy is necessary.

One of the difficulties in treating this disturbance is the extreme seductiveness of the patients, which results in considerable countertransference. The patient communicates a very compelling level of need and a deep positive investment in the relationship. Then there are unexpected acting out behaviors (running away, stealing from the therapist, doing malicious damage) which reveal little sincere investment in the relationship. Therapists are advised to become involved in these relationships with caution and avoid any excessive caretaking.

Catatonia

Catatonia is characterized by a gross behavioral slowdown often interspersed with periods of violence or running. These behaviors, along with a possibility of suicide, are answers to the question "How do I get away from this not-OK world?" Often the dynamics are disguised by an hysterical overlay. Persistent attempts at withdrawal and a waxy appearance are the most easily recognized symtoms.

Any demand for meaningful personal involvement is seen as a threat to existence. This is because it directly threatens the patients' control of withdrawal. They view "letting someone in" as giving that person direct control over their survival. This is, however, the only course for treatment to take. Stroking can sometimes elicit voluntary involvement because of the urgency with which the patients experience strokehunger; however, involvement in the early stages is likely to wax and wane, even within optimum circumstances. Success with two nonvoluntary patients was achieved with much coaxing and prodding.

Since the disturbance originates in early infancy as a result of negative and unpredictable interactions with the environment, it is important that the patients be physically stroked, held, and reassured. The fixation occurs in the latter part of infancy when the infants experience themselves as unable to make anything work and fail to develop the expectation that they will be able to control and run the world. The control struggle, which is characteristic of the third year, is then internalized and acted out as an internal mechanism. This conflict is elaborated during the eight- to twelve-year-old stage, and constant hassling may be experienced by the therapist. The hassling represents an attempt at withdrawing under the guise of relating. The patients should be stopped from hassling and encouraged to relate spontaneously to the situation.

Birth is an important issue. The child wishes to have never been born, and regression is to the last period of comfort, the time of prebirth. The decision to be born and, thereby, to give up the withdrawal, is often acted out over and over, and the decision to live in the world is eventually based on a trust that things will be better in the world as presented by the therapist.

There may be an eating disturbance (anorexia) and it is important for the patient to identify the suicidal nature of that. A *no suicide* and *no running* contract is required. Frequently physical restraint is requested or required, confirming that running is not an option. Therapists working successfully with these patients report much involvement in very primitive control struggles (e.g., wrestling, restraint, and force feeding).

A preliminary diagram of the catatonic structure shows the person's Child ego state divided into three functional areas as in Figure 17.

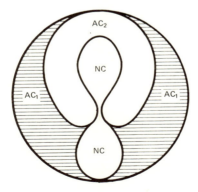

FIG. 17. Catatonia

There is a set of Adapted Child behaviors, AC_1, which are socially appropriate, as well as a set of pathological behaviors which encapsulate the discounted Natural Child behaviors, feelings, needs, and wants. These pathological adaptations act as a permeable energy barrier surrounding the discounted Natural Child. In some circumstances access to the discounted Child through this barrier is relatively easy, while in others the barrier appears impermeable. However, in most circumstances access is gained most easily by identifying and responding to aspects of the Natural Child not encapsulated by AC_2.

Paranoia

Paranoia occurs when the patient habitually escalates anger over fear. There is a script injunction against permitting the feeling of fear, and a prescription recommending extreme anger as an appropriate response to fearful situations. In schizophrenia, paranoid type, a Parent contamination is used to maintain the angry righteous position. Also, the Adult is misinformed, in that it is the patient's belief that people are immobilized with fear in such a way as to totally incapacitate around any problem-solving. The misinformation may be further complicated by delusions (Child contamination) during acute episodes.

Developmentally the disturbance appears to have begun in the middle part of the oral stage (8-15 months). As the infant becomes mobile, is teething, eating solids, smearing feces, etc., the mother (or other primary source of nurturing) responds with guilt about not liking the infant and withdrawal (experienced by the Child as rejection). The Child learns to circumvent the rejection by eliciting a guilty response (Rescue) and thus learns preference for the Victim position in the Karpman Drama Triangle. The mother generally reinforces the preference for the Victim position in her assumption of a martyr role (Victim defending Persecutor), often competing with the Child for the Victim position.

The Child is taught to escalate feelings in a variety of ways. There are two basic positions, both reinforcing a not-OK victim stance: the low-level suffer (whine, physical disabilities, "Ain't it Awful!") and the crisis. The dynamics of each position are taught separately. For instance, the whine is paid off when the child is taken out of the play pen or crib after extended periods of low-level suffering, and the crisis or high-level escalation may be taught by tickling until the child is hysterical.

In doing regressive work, it is always evident that the regressed baby is not-OK and suffering. Generally the individual has extreme difficulty relinguishing bladder control and will endure excruciating pain caused by withholding urination (this rarely occurs at a significant level in other pathologies). When there is spontaneous cathexis to Child in a paranoid patient, the suffering is demonstrated as blubbering, nose running, and drooling. This is done to an extent that an unsympathetic, rejecting response is often experienced from the therapist or group. They are likely to respond with guilt, over-adaptation, and nurturing, thus duplicating the original situation.

A more therapeutic response is to notice the suffering, respond with immediate nurturing plus criticism, provide the care the behavior is eliciting, and make it clear that the not-OK behavior is unnecessary and unacceptable. The patient should be reassured that rejection is not a possibility. "Stop blubbering; you don't have to be not-OK to get taken care of. We aren't going to reject you."

An important dynamic in paranoia is "the secret." The secret is an oedipal fantasy which a hurt and scared five-year-old boy or girl constructs to explain why the mother doesn't like him or her. Animalistic identification is a likely part of this fantasy.

Example: a patient who was called a "little monkey" believed she was part ape; another, who was called "a son of a bitch" expected to become a wolf. Despite evidence to the contrary, patients who seem not significantly delusional will cling to these fantasies. Most pathological behaviors are behaviors adapted to defend against acting out the fantasy. This defense mechanism can be effectively represented to patients as a Bubble on the Child ego state. This is not meant to be structural or theoretically rigorous. Thus, we describe the paranoid as having a set of socially appropriate behaviors, AC_1 (See Fig. 18), a set of socially inappropriate behaviors, AC_2 (both of which are defenses against the Bubble), and a set of bizarre behaviors related to the animalistic fantasy in the Bubble.

Many Natural Child wants, needs, and feelings are closeted in the Bubble and are defined by the patient as not-OK. We have experienced positive results by having the patients cathect into the Bubble fantasy, confronting the craziness (or silliness) of their behavior, and persuading

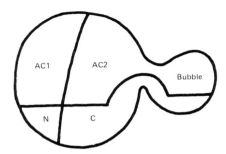

FIG. 18. The Paranoid Bubble

them to maintain cathexis there so we may make direct contact with the Natural Child.

At a non-psychotic level paranoia is commonly called a "Kick Me" game. These patients elicit negative responses from therapists and groups from a seemingly naive position. The "Kick Me" structure results from an internal redefinition of strokes so that negative strokes are experienced as positive as well as negative. This stroke manipulation is delusional and difficult to confront in treatment because it is rarely transactionally identifiable. The patient needs to learn to identify positive strokes as significant in order to give up the need for negative strokes.

Hysteria

The Hysteric personality is characterized by emotional outbursts, overadaptation, an apparent, often feigned, shallowness, and exaggerated attention to appearances issues.

It appears that many of these characteristics develop in the mid-oral stage where the child is expected to be cute, sweet, pretty, well-behaved, and generally live up to the mother's fantasy of what the baby should be like. By adapting to that expectation the child learns to take care of mother/others in order to get needs met.

The functional diagram of the Hysteric's Child (See Fig. 19) serves to explain many phenomena encountered with these individuals.

The Hysteric tends to discount Natural Child feelings and move into an overadapted or adapted position instead of dealing with the experienced feelings. This mechanism derives from such P_2 messages as "Be

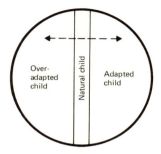

FIG. 19. *Hysteria*

Strong" and "Look Good" and from such injunctions as, "Don't Show Feelings," and "Don't Think."

The Hysteric perceives Natural Child feelings, wants, and needs as not-OK and therefore tends to avoid either being in touch with or expressing them. Instead, operating from a fantasy of external expectations, the hysteric strives to please, be efficient, and look good. Since these operations involve frustration of Natural Child needs, suppressed anger builds in the Overadapted Child. The characteristic angry outbursts provide a release for this energy and are seen as Adapted Child behaviors. Typically, the repertoire of Adapted Child behaviors elicits a negative response from others and validates the existential position "There's no way to get my needs met."

After the Adapted Child escalation, it appears that Natural Child is available for parenting. The goal in treatment is to persuade the Hysteric to cathect out of Overadapted Child and into the Adapted Child pathology. The dysfunctional behaviors, in particular redefining transactions, are confronted, and the patient is expected to define and meet needs without relating to the dysfunctional adaptations.

Manic-Depressive

The manic depressive disturbance is illustrated in Figure 20.

The major dynamic is that because of the competitive frame of reference in the family where a particular function can only be done by one member of the family, any capacity for successfully doing things which are done by others is denied. Since feelings are often the functional property of another member of the family, the expression of Na-

FIG. 20. *Manic-Depressive*

tural Child becomes an overwhelming problem at times when environmental stress elicits feelings. Additionally, anger and fright are serious problems to the patient who can only express them within the structure of pathological escalations (from an "I'm not doing anything" position).

Developmentally, the most significant issue is a competition between the nurturing person and the Child over who is going to avoid the agitation. This continues as the Child grows, complicated by confusing and inconsistent Parent messages around doing things. An example which is experienced as meaningful by nearly all these patients is being spoon fed. Generally these children are fed by others well beyond the stage in which most babies feed themselves, and the feedings present a high level conflict resulting in agitation for either the child or the parent. When the patients are manic they are perceived by others as very agitated; they state they feel fine. However, people around them are likely to experience a great deal of agitation.

The role of females is generally to rescue, and strokes are likely to be perceived only from the Victim position when rescued externally. Sex is important but only available as meaningful in bizarre or grandiose contexts.

The issue is existence and the very limited options available to the patients to establish their existence. Treatment consists of broadening the options for recognition around doing things, both by increasing skills and by supporting these people in setting goals, pursuing those goals successfully, and recognizing this accomplishment. These individuals discount external reality at a high level, which facilitates the discounting of accomplishments and also serves as an expression of power within the context of a competitive frame of reference. This is important to confront, as the doing things issue cannot be approached successfully until the patients have some awareness of reality.

Obsessive-Compulsive

A major characteristic of the family backgrounds of obsessive-compulsive patients is the long-distance quarrels. Family members will stand in separate rooms and shout at one another. This is significant in view of the patients' considerable fear of closeness and their own angry or violent impulses. However, these are projected away from the self and onto the external environment.

Developmentally, this disturbance is like paranoia in origin, the major difference being that nurturing person compensated the rejecting impulses by becoming overprotective.

Nurturing, anger, and fear are important issues. Physical stroking and holding are very important in treatment, and as the patient begins to get permission to have feelings and still be close, largely as a result of the therapist's willingness to do that, the angry impulses begin to emerge and be dealt with. Treatment of these issues appears to be relatively easy. A problem in treatment is that often therapists have difficulty overcoming impulses to withdraw from the patients, whom they perceive as not appealing.

Depression

Depression as we are considering it here is seen as a condition characterized by emotion dejection and withdrawal beyond that warranted by the situation. As a mechanism, it involves a general slowdown of responses and an inhibition of both internal experience of stimuli and the responses to them, either affectual or behavioral.

Doing things is a focal point in the frame of reference. The specific difficulty in doing things varies with individuals as a script issue, but the general problem is the same: people experience themselves as either unable, unwilling, or uninterested in doing things. The unwillingness is the more honest position and more direct expression of the negativism, but it is often true that some people eventually may become so depressed that they are not able to do things without external support. The negativism may represent a lack of resolution in the socialization conflict between age two and three. Since these people know that the anger is not appropriate and the expression will only result in a negative or discounting response from the environment, depression becomes the preferred alternative. Other feelings, such as fear or grief, may be the source of the difficulty. Treatment is slow, since the initial problem involves getting the patients active enough to begin dealing with the actual issues. This requires continual prodding, encouragement, rescuing, and the use of negative and positive strokes (though the latter are likely to be discounted). Eventually the negativism or other issues will emerge and be available to treatment if the treatment structure provides resources the patients recognize as relevant.

Character Disorders

Individuals with a character disordered personality have either incorporated minimal Parent ego state or have incorporated an atypical Parent. To compensate for the inadequate incorporation of Parent, A_2 and A_1 are seen as highly developed. Thus, behavior is often controlled by relating to issue-specific consequences rather than to any generalized Parent value structure. The patients with a character disordered personality also use Witch Parent mechanisms to scare themselves into appropriate behaviors (See Chapter Four, "Fearful Fours"). The issues for those with character disorders then become, "Is there some way I can figure out how to get away with this?" or "Is this too scary to try?"

Unlike the schizophrenic who experienced an unhealthy symbiosis, those with character disorders never fully established a primary symbiosis—separation from the mother or inconsistency being a probable cause.

Inadequate Personality

Some patients survived the first few years of life without serious disorder and then experienced some external trauma, such as the death of a parent and a drastic change in life experience, to which the child was unable to adapt. Fixation occurred and eventually the child became socially dysfunctional, generally as a result of omitted parenting (strokes or discipline being the most common problems). When the omitted parenting and experience is identified and supplied, the individual can move ahead.

Phobias

The phobic person is irrationally afraid of objects or events. His reaction to these tend to be withdrawal and the adoption of an appealing, somewhat helpless position. The person experiences difficulties in structuring time and energy, doing things, and being involved in the world. The fear is escalated hysterically as an avoidance mechanism. These individuals attempt to maintain a passive dependent position in relation to the world and use their fear as a justification for this. Essentially these patients incapacitate because they don't think they can do anything.

Treatment consists of insisting on the patients being active and involved in whatever activity they select. There is a lot of attention given to time structuring and on teaching the patients what to do and how do do it in different situations. The aim is to increase their skills in relating to the world adequately, and there is an ongoing expansion of expectations for involvement with it.

Other Problems

Alcoholism, drug abuse, and sexual deviance are typical of a class of problems seen as defense structures covering underlying pathology. These adaptations derive from the individual's script injunctions and messages as well as from behavior seen in parent models.

Treatment involves identifying the underlying dynamics and dealing with the underlying dynamics directly.

Chapter Seven

REPARENTING AND REGRESSION

REPARENTING

Definition

Reparenting is a method used in the treatment of psychosis. It involves the total decathexis of the originally incorporated Parent ego state, and the replacement of that structure with a new Parent structure.

This replacement process is facilitated by the psychotics' ability to totally and permanently decathect the originally incorporated Parent ego state. This decathexis of Parent is seen as a Child decision to remove all energy (bound and unbound)[13] from the Parent. These individuals perceive themselves as having no available Parent. The energy removed from the Parent is then available for incorporating the new Parent. Some energy is released in this process, since energizing the defense structure against threats of the old Parent is no longer necessary.

The Parent contains all the definitional parameters within which these people function (frame of reference) and removal of these leaves them vulnerable.

Full decathexis of Parent is not desirable unless there is a sufficiently supportive external structure upon which these people can rely. In addition, if the individuals do not perceive the environment as capable of supporting a full decathexis of Parent, the loss of structure they anticipate may preclude a full decathexis of Parent. They are then likely to keep sufficient Parent available to facilitate functioning within the

---

13. Berne, *Transactional Analysis in Psychotherapy*, pp. 40-41.

environment. Another mode of reparenting has been developed which allows for these factors and is used primarily in outpatient settings where full support of decathexis of Parent is not possible.

In an outpatient setting, individuals gradually exclude old Parent by removing, in stepwise fashion, unbound (functionally used) energy in the Parent, leaving bound energy (structure) intact. Thus, old Parent *structure* remains as a resource to maintain stability of energy, but is not functionally used. New Parent structure is then gradually incorporated. When sufficient new Parent structure has been incorporated for the patients to use it alone, it becomes practical to fully decathect the formerly excluded old Parent. This overall process involves a more gradual reorganization of the individuals' frame of reference.

Motivation for Decathexis

Both psychotic and nonpsychotic frames of reference are seen as adaptive structures for the Natural Child. The frame of reference had survival value in the primary family, and therefore considerable investment even in dysfunctional frames of reference is often seen. This explains, at least in part, why patients may experience considerable conflict over decathecting their Parent. Though uncomfortable, its past survival value may eclipse the discomfort experienced.

Decisions to change frame of reference derive from Natural Child. Thus, fantasized gratification from use of the new frame of reference, along with information, reassurance, and support from the new parent figures is important in an individual's decision to de-invest energizing the old Parent structure. The more dysfunctional the frame of reference, the less positive investment the individual is likely to have in the Parent that contains the definitional parameters for that frame of reference. Thus, if the individual's frame of reference proves dysfunctional through reality testing, there is likely to be little investment in maintaining that structure.

Nonpsychotic Applications

The facility for full decathexis of Parent is not seen in nonpsychotic patients. For the nonpsychotic individual, the definitional parameters provided by the originally incorporated Parent allows for a frame of reference that is somewhat functional and correspondingly gratifying. To the degree that the frame of reference is experienced as functional, the derived gratification provides positive reinforcement for maintaining the incorporated Parent structure. This investment in the Parent structure may therefore preclude full decathexis of that structure. The treatment problem then becomes one of filling in gaps in the extant Parent structure by providing new specific Parent messages, definitions, and reasons to effect modifications of the person's frame of reference. This process is called Parenting.

Parenting

When used with nonpsychotic patients, parenting does not require a full decathexis of Parent. The frame of reference is modified by providing specific Parent messages, definitions, and reasons to effect change in the frame of reference. It is important that the Parent messages given relate to all three ego states to affect an integrated frame of reference. Thus, reasons and information must be given in relation to the Parent messages (Adult), and Child adaptations must be taught and reinforced through experience. If the new Parent messages are inconsistent with reality data, Child adaptations to that message may not prove gratifying, reinforcement for adaptation to the message will not occur, and the individual may discount the new message.

In parenting, the individual can use fantasy to discount certain Parent messages. The process, often referred to as "caging the Parent" involves the individual having a fantasy of locking up the Parent ego state in a cage. Functionally, the person selectively discounts old Parent messages. If the new messages, reasons, and adaptations prove gratifying, the individual will persist in discounting the old messages and continue energizing the new Parent construct.

Symbiosis

Decathexis, selective discounting or exclusion of Parent, involves the person imposing a symbiosis on others. For effective treatment to occur, the therapist enters into the symbiosis, when parenting or reparenting, to facilitate the patient's working through the symbioses and reaching autonomy. When a regression is involved, reparenting is done in the context of normal childhood development where Child needs are met; Parent messages, definitions, and limits are incorporated; and Adult data learned.

REGRESSION

Regression has become an important process and valuable tool in the treatment of psychotic disorders. In fact, it is doubtful if the success which has been achieved would have been possible without utilizing this characteristic of the disturbance fully.

Definitions

Psychotic regression is a process in which the Child is cathected at a very young age (usually prior to one year), identifiable physiological changes occur, and regression is locked in the sense that the person cannot cathect a Natural, i.e., spontaneously reactive, Child ego state older than the regressed age. It is this sense of the term regression which will be used most often in this writing.

Nonpsychotic regressions appear to be of three distinct but related types: (1) Pseudo-regression is a process which initially appears to be a full psychotic regression but does not become locked in the way that psychotic regressions do, and patients can cathect out of the regression (and usually do). This may occur because these people are not psychotic and therefore do not have available to them the mechanisms required, or because they have not made the requisite decision to utilize those mechanisms. (2) Regression as a temporary cathexis to Child at a given age is a process in which the patients shift a large quantity of energy to the Child ego state and only use energy for the Parent and Adult to the degree appropriate to the age cathected. (3) Adaptive regression is the process in which patients respond to an environmental stimulus or complex of stimuli by a relatively or absolutely fixed cathexis to Child. This phenomena may be observed in the case of people who have been rendered nonfunctional as a result of physical trauma and in nursing homes where elderly patients respond to the enforced dependency with an adaptive cathexis to Child. In the latter case there are also likely to be physiological components to the regression as well as psychological.

Dynamics of Regression

Regression in psychotic patients occurs in response to either internal or external stress which may or may not be objective. That is, these people may not be experiencing the stress in response to some part of public reality but rather in response to their own interpretation from a deviant or maladaptive frame of reference. The stress may be almost exclusively internal when the personality is so disorganized that these individuals are only occupied with delusional or hallucinating experience. On the other hand, the stress may be as a result of an external situation which requires them to respond in a way or at a level of which they are either incapable, or which would violate primary script injunctions and thereby threaten existence.

Regression is a decisional process. In response to stress people decide to utilize physiological mechanisms not usually available and decide to reactivate both very young Child experiences and responses. They essentially become an infant again. Regression is usually accompanied by marked physiological changes: women often stop menstruating, men will frequently cease to ejaculate, and sometimes there will be a reactivation of infantile reflexes. Many secondary sex characteristics, however, are not changed, such as the beard growth in males. Nevertheless, in very regressive persons many of those characteristics will not have developed fully or at all.

Though regression is a result of a decision by the Child, once the decision is made and the process begun, the patients cannot halt its progress. They may cathect away from the regressed Child and utilize other ego states, but they cannot cathect a spontaneously reactive Child older than the regressed age.

There are four structures typical of regression:

1. Parent de-cathected
2. Parent excluded: Partial or total
3. Adult excluded: Partial or total
4. No exclusion

> 1. Parent de-cathected: This structure is most often seen in a supportive treatment situation familiar with and utilizing the techniques developed at Cathexis Institute. Occasionally patients will discover this procedure themselves, in which case they are likely to appear as a character disorder.
>
> Structurally these people have only an Adult and a Child ego state. This generally is not a good position from which to start a regression since the Child is still usually disturbed and the pathology is likely to interfere with the therapeutic usefulness of the regression.

2. Parent excluded: Usually people will exclude the Parent ego state, at least in the early stages of the regression, either because it is a pathological structure perceived as detrimental to the Child's safety and/or welfare, or if they have been reparented and have a new Parent ego state, it will be inconsistent with their experiences as an infant to cathect an ego state as developmentally mature as the Parent. Sometimes the exclusion is only partial with the Parent being cathected only occasionally or selectively. This may be the case with individuals who are sufficiently confused or disorganized as to make stability of cathexis difficult or impossible. It may also be the case in a supported regression when there are major issues of trust of the new mother left unresolved before undertaking the regression. Additionally, the exclusion may be only partial by contract when it is necessary for a person in a supported regression to maintain occasional and limited functioning at a more mature level; hence, the use of the other ego states.

3. Adult excluded: The Adult is usually excluded for much the same reasons as the Parent. It is perceived as either detrimental to or discrepant with the Child. It is also unlikely that the patients will be able to cathect an uncontaminated Adult, at least in the very early stages of regression prior to two years of age. Once again the exclusion may only be partial for the same reasons as with the Parent.

4. No ego state excluded: If the patients are sufficiently disorganized they may not be able or may not choose to exclude the Parent or the Adult (which would be very contaminated). This situation may be observed in patients with long-term hospitalization which has reinforced acting crazy as a survival mechanism. Also within a supportive structure, occasionally patients may regress without prior arrangement or contract and have to continue to function but this is usually only possible if they already have a functional Parent and a relatively uncontaminated Adult.

Internally, the Child responds to stress on the basis of an anal decision made in reaction to the demands and pressures of the socialization conflict at about age two (See Chapter Four). Two apparently conflicting decisions are made at that time: one to get as much as quickly as

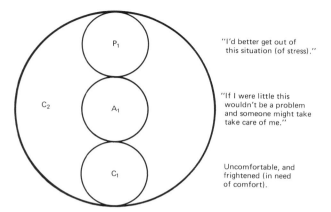

FIG. 21. *Immediately Prior to Regression*

possible to reduce the dependency through which the Child is vulnerable to the demands of the Parent; the other that the Child would rather be helpless than face the conflict which promises so little gratification in its resolution since the Child's relationship with the mother is already unsatisfactory. The seeming conflict is not experienced as a significant reality problem since the second decision only becomes relevant at higher levels of stress. The first is most often used to defend against the second by attempting to deny the feelings and needs of the Child. Figure 21 structurally diagrams the second decision at the time of regression.

The somatic Child, C_1, controls the initiation of the physiology of regression. This is done in response to a sufficient level of discomfort when P_1 and A_1 identify the situation as sufficiently threatening and there do not appear to be other viable options. In relation to the external environment, regression is an attempt to illicit a symbiotic response which will get the Child taken care of in some manner, though perhaps not the kind of care that is needed. Internally it is an attempt to alleviate discomfort by cathecting an ego state to which the stressful stimuli are meaningless.

Regression as a Therapeutic Technique

There have been attempts in the past to utilize psychotic regression as a therapeutic tool. However, they have met with limited success, and there has been little recognition of the value of supporting the regressive aspect of psychotic disturbances. For the most part regression has been viewed with alarm and distaste. Patients were told that the behaviors were pathological, unacceptable, and destructive. Perhaps it was true that regression in the setting of a state hospital or comparable institution was destructive. Virtually no one was willing to accept or even listen to the patients' claim that their needs were legitimate and had to be met before they could successfully mature to a healthy adulthood. Those who did accept it were all too often unwilling to provide the requisite structure and involvement. Moreover, institutions are not optimal places to rear young children.

The characteristics of supported and nonsupported regression are usually quite markedly different. Typically regressed patients in a nonsupportive environment will be perceived as acting quite bizarrely, with no distinction between "acting crazy" and presenting behaviors and responses consistent with the needs of a young infant. The patients may not clearly distinguish them either since much of the "crazy behavior" is an attempt to elicit some response from an environment which consistently discounts them. The picture presented by a regressed person in an environment which is designed to provide support and protection, and to respond to those needs is quite different. At first glance the behaviors will appear unusual because of the discrepancy between the physical size, anticipated maturity, and the manifestation of the infantile needs. Most observers, however, quickly adjust to the discrepancy and can easily respond to the person as a baby or child, not as someone acting crazy.

The requirements for supporting a regression vary with the degree to which it is possible, desirable, or necessary to support it. Roughly the distinction would be between fully supported, partially supported, and outpatient programs. For a fully supported regression a protective environment with continual supervision (at least in the initial stages) is needed, with a clearly established parent figure in the nurturing role to fulfill the conditions of the symbiosis. It is likely that this should be a woman, though the issue is not completely settled. The most conducive setting would be a family where the person already has a strong positive relationship with the new mother and father. Other arrangements are possible, usually, however, with some reduction of effectiveness. In a partially supported regression it is necessary to provide a structure such as those described above for the first two developmental years after which the person may resume some degree of more mature functioning on a limited scale. In order to maintain functioning that person will need to "be little" and to make a full cathexis to Child for at least part of every day. If this is not done, there usually will be an escalation of pathology within a week, as the person moves into either a compensation or overt "craziness." Both reactions are therapeutically counterproductive. The results of partial support are not as therapeutically thoroughgoing or usually as dramatic since issues will have been left unresolved due to the limitation on the time spent in full cathexis to Child. Though working with regression on an outpatient basis is not a recommended procedure, it is nevertheless necessary on occasion. In the event a patient regresses without a contract (and all regressive patients should be told not to do this, and the message reinforced), the therapist must choose to provide as much support as possible. This would normally require at least daily contact with either the therapist or other nurturing figure in order to meet some of the infant needs and to support the person in continued functioning. The results in this situation are not likely to be very therapeutic, but it may be possible to keep the patient out of a hospital situation which might be more damaging. For these reasons it is important for the person to incorporate clear prohibitions against regressing without a contract and a structure adequate to provide care.

In contrast, however, regressive techniques can be used on an outpatient basis quite successfully. Utilizing a program which permits the person to cathect Child for several hours regularly three to five times a week, many patients can be maintained without hospitalization and unproductive regression avoided. In this situation the young needs are being met, and the structure provides a release so that the stress level does not exceed the patient's tolerance (See Chapter Eight).

Psychotic regression will usually be to an age prior to the beginning of the pathology, prior to one year of age. The person will then proceed through the developmental sequence of maturation at an average rate of one developmental year per three to six weeks. The typical pattern is to present the maladaptive or pathological behaviors to obtain negative reinforcement and some level of extinction, then to move into the same areas of development to acquire new experience which is more consonant with the welfare and eventual success of the person. It is important that the therapist be willing to provide the negative feedback required since often the patient cannot define the areas of maladaptive behaviors.

This chapter by no means exhausts the information on regression or its therapeutic use, but it does provide the basic information about the structure, dynamics, and support of regression. Hopefully, more programs will be established which utilize the regressive characteristic of many psychotic disturbances as a therapeutic tool and which recognize it as perhaps the healthiest option available to these individuals.

Chapter Eight

TREATMENT PHILOSOPHY

Underpinning our interventions with patients is a consciously formulated and experientially supported philosophy. Two major components are that patients know cognitively and/or viscerally what they need to do to get well, and that they can take responsibility for their functioning during treatment if they have a supportive environment while they develop new internal structures and options for behavior. Our treatment structure and interventions are programmed in relation to these ideas.

Psychotic patients have consistently demonstrated that they will escalate behaviors related to problems. This is generally in the desperate hope that someone external will define, understand, and confront the problem which the patient, because of a thinking disorder, is unable to resolve. The behaviors are considered to be immediately symptomatic of the problem or to be part of the patient's structure of defenses to avoid the problem.

Example: a hebephrenic patient, presented with the task of doing a jigsaw puzzle is likely to become very upset and agitated, usually about some issue irrelevant to the task.

By confronting the behaviors, the underlying pathology or needs are exposed and can be dealt with. This presumes, of course, a treatment structure and staff willing to deal with the pathology. Frequently, given such a structure and staff, the patients are able to conceptualize what they need and make plans with the staff for solving problems. Transactional analysis is used as a unifying theory of personality and communication to facilitate the thinking of patients and staff.

Additionally, we see patients, especially those with incapacitating thinking, emotional, and behavioral disturbances, as individuals whose life experiences have not adequately prepared them for autonomous coping. They have learned a number of dysfunctional ways of behaving, and these represent major options for problem-solving. However, most of them are in touch with an imperative drive to get well, and in an environment which is strongly antithetical to pathological behavior and strongly promotes autonomous problem-solving, the drive for health flourishes. Patients rapidly begin to incorporate new and more functional thinking, feeling, acting, and problem-solving adaptations.

It is significant to our philosophy that we use structure instead of medication. As a research organization, we have found that medication sufficiently confuses affectual and behavioral reactions so as to seriously interfere with our goals. Moreover, we have found no justification for the utilization of medication related to the patients' welfare and social functioning. During the course of treatment this continues to be true as long as the patient has ongoing contact with an environment which does not reinforce the pathological games and consistently confronts discounts.

All of our patients have unmet needs from early in life when normal cognitive and affectual development was thwarted. Their level and kinds of functioning are often equivalent to that of a child. In planning an environment to provide sufficient support for such individuals, we have found it advantageous to set expectations according to the patients' capacity for healthy functioning and not their chronological age. While patients are expected to behave in socially appropriate ways outside the treatment structure, within the protected environment they may freely become children of an age where they can engage in spontaneous problem-solving with adequate protection (cathexis to Child). Chronological age becomes irrelevant, and frequently it seems almost that we are running a nursery school for oversized toddlers. With this kind of support, patients no longer have to "hold things together" and can devote energy to more relevant problem-solving.

The treatment structure is Parent programmed. We believe it is impossible to teach people how to live without giving them value-oriented definitions by which to live. Representative Parent messages are: "You are responsible for what you say and do," "There are always reasons," "Feelings are OK," "You can solve problems," "You are expected to think," and "It is not OK to discount yourself, others, or reality." Basic to our general structure is an assumption that there is an objective reality which people can observe and mutually define. This empirical position is adopted consciously knowing that there may be philosophical and experiential exceptions taken on some points. We consider this approach essential to patients until they are well along in treatment, because statements such as "No one can know what you are feeling, or thinking unless you show them by what you do or say," and "No, I don't disappear when you go into the next room" and "It's not OK to tell lies," address very real issues related to existence and identity for our patient population. Philosophical hedging and speculation is avoided until later in favor of a clear statement which can be used by our patients in their day-to-day functioning.

Through exposure to this structure patients are encouraged to incorporate a new Parent ego state. Positive support is also given to the development of new, functional Child adaptations with which patients are enabled to define themselves internally and cope with social demands. To this end it is important that the life-style promoted within the therapeutic structure be compatible with that of the surrounding community. This facilitates the patients' making the translations necessary for adequate functioning as they move away from treatment structures and into the larger society. Most patients have to put energy into this process because they tend to use their incorporated structures rigidly (as do children at particular ages) until they find out what really works and have become brave enough to begin experimentation. Inflexibility presents a substantial treatment problem. Many of the patients, having found something which works (even imperfectly), are unwilling to consider the possibility that they have not yet acquired the optimum, ultimate answer, and that they must keep thinking and changing as they encounter new life experiences.

An important aspect of our therapeutic structure is the reactiveness of the environment. Throughout our society, people learn to discount various aspects of their own and other people's behavior in the interest of conflict-free relating. The result is that many people are unaware of the effect they have on others, and when they have problems in behaving appropriately, the problems are often discounted. Crazy behavior is often the result of such discounting since the only option many dysfunctional individuals perceive is to escalate inappropriate behavior until it can no longer be discounted. This is particularly true since such individuals generally do not have information about nurturing or caring responses in others. These responses were not a significant part of their experience, and consequently these individuals are uncertain as to how to capture awareness from others in what seems to them a competition for recognition to confirm existence. In addition, they feel the recognition needed must be elicited from a basically rejecting world.

The results of this problem are often bizarre. In a reactive environment where the goal is to confront all appearances of pathology, we find that even the most sick people "act crazy" only a small proportion of the time and then usually only to work out a problem. There is a clear inverse relationship between the level of craziness and the level of confrontation. When one is high, the other is low.

In order to insure that the constant level of external feedback is maintained, staff and patients alike are expected to make a commitment to a general confrontation contract. The contract is to confront and be confronted from a caring position. Caring may be for the self, or for the person being confronted. Caring for oneself simply involves a statement, "What you are doing makes me uncomfortable. I want you to stop that and. . . ." This is based on an assumption that people who are interacting do have an effect on one another and can be held responsible for that effect. It is also considered all right to confront from a position of caring for the other person, i.e., "I think it is too bad that you are doing that, because it won't turn out well for you," but those transactions need to be viewed carefully for the possibility of shifted feelings or other symbiotic content.

Confrontation which makes the person not all right is, in itself, confronted as an inappropriate expression of hostility. Each confrontation is expected to be specific about the behaviors involved, the feelings the person making the confrontation is having, and there is an expectation for an appropriate response. The person being confronted is expected to think about the issues and respond appropriately. That person should take responsibility for those behaviors which are agreed to be inappropriate by coming to understand the game involved, dealing with the other person in a way which facilitates future relating, and making a clear commitment to specified change.

Contracts are considered to be important. However, many of our patients, in the initial phase of treatment, are sufficiently dysfunctional as to make a general treatment contract meaningless. For this reason we are likely to start out with a "soft" contract, and at a later time make the contract more specific, or break it into mini-contracts as the treatment proceeds.

Major exchanges of power occur in therapeutic relationships. Patients often wish to invest therapists with authority and responsibility which the therapists are unwilling to accept. Our policy is to accept the patients' investment of power (transference) to the extent we believe it possible to utilize that power for their welfare. Generally our philosophy that the patients know what they need is considered relevant. If the power is useful in developing capacity for relating and trusting and accepting nurturing, that can certainly be considered desirable. If games are involved, we can confront them, and the patients can learn through the experience. Perhaps what the patients need is to give away the power so that they can struggle in order to recover it. Whatever is motivating the attempt to form the symbiosis, we would consider it more appropriate to do something than to do nothing with the feelings and needs involved. Ultimately, of course, the power is restored to the patients, although if the transference has been complete, the relationships may have ongoing significance.

Finally, in treatment, all facets of life and living are seen as potentially relevant. Cathexis Institute is increasingly known for its use of regressive techniques which are based on a theory of child development and the genesis of pathology related to specific developmental stages. However, the focus and theoretical framework is much broader. Cultural, social, psychodynamic, and biological factors each may become the specific focus of treatment. The perspective may be to relate them to here and now phenomena or to past experiences and future projections.

Our staff suggested that the following quote from Lord Buckley be used to describe our ideas about therapeutic intervention: *"If you get to it, and you cannot do it, there you jolly well are, aren't you?"*[14] We operate from a basic position that it is OK to get to it, and then we are supposed to do something. Often what we do matters less than our willingness to be involved, to enter into the struggle with the patients,

---

14. *The Best of Lord Buckley* (Los Angeles: Vaya Records, 1951).

to lend them our resources of energy and thinking when their own fail, and to reinforce their autonomy when they are able to function. We don't think it is necessary to be nice to the patients if niceness interferes with clarity. We doubt that it is possible for anyone to get well while maintaining an unreal investment in comfort, the comfort of either the patient or the therapists. We deal in issues as primitive as vomiting, feces, and violence, and we try to deal with them in sensible and sensitive ways. We use all of our personal resources and are willing to address all of the patients' needs which we can understand and respond to.

In starting to write this chapter a detailed list was developed of all the things we do. We then decided that the specifics, which are constantly changing as our staff changes and our ideas become clarified, are irrelevant to the purpose of this book. The concept of intervention, injecting ourselves between the patients and their ineffective operations with their environment in a forceful and caring way, describes what we try to do. When we are successful it is exciting and we learn. When we fail, it is unfortunate, and we still learn. There is a lot we already know, and much still to discover.

INDEX

Index

A

Active behavior, 10
Adaptation, 11, 40, 42, 89, 99, 100
    Parent and Adult as, 24, 26
    thinking as an, 22, 24
Adaptive regression, *see* Regression, types of
Adolescent stage, *see* Developmental stages
Adult ego state, 22, 23, 25
    cathexis of, 24, 41
    decathexis of, 31
    exclusion of, 30, 93
    in frame of reference, 26
Adulthood, young, *see* Developmental stages
Agitation, 8, 10, 12-13, 33-34, 36, 47, 74
    manic depressive, 84
    in redefining, 65
    shifts in, 12-13, 36
All My Children, 3
Anal resolution, 22
    See also The Terrible Twos
Anal stage, *see* Developmental stages, The Terrible Twos
Anger, 7, 8, 11, 40, 79-80, 85, 86
Angry Righteous, *see* Redefining, roles
Angry Wrongdoer, *see* Redefining, roles

Areas of discounting, 14-17
Awareness, 6, 18, 19

B

Behaviors, passive, *see* Passive behaviors; Passivity syndrome
Berne, Eric, 6, 19, 24
Birth, 79
    See also Developmental stages
"The Bubble," *see* Pathological structures, paranoia

C

"Caging the Parent," *see* Reparenting
Caretaker, *see* Redefining, roles
Caring, 101
Catatonia, *see* Pathological structures
Cathexis, 26, 47-48
    Adult, 24
    and developmental stage, 47-48
    pathways of, in frame of reference, 50-51
Cathexis Institute, 1-4
    description, vii
    general goals, 1, 4
Cathexis School, 3, 4
    See also Outpatient structure

Character disorder, *see* Pathological structures
Child development, 32-48
 changes of symbiosis in, 34, 37, 39, 41, 42-43, 43-44, 45, 46
Child ego state, 24
 decathexis of, 30-31
 exclusion of, 30
 in frame of reference, 26, 51
Communication, frame of reference in, 52
Competition, 19, 44, 59, 73-74
 antithesis, 74
 in frame of reference, *see* Frame of reference, competitive
 for game position, 68
 manic depressive, 83-84
 over symbiosis, 7-8, 60
  redefining relationships, 62-65, 68
Contamination, 8, 17, 27-29, 53, 59
 redefining in, 58
 in symbiosis, 60-65
Conditional strokes, *see* Strokes
Confrontation, 101
Contracts, *see* Treatment
Counter-transference, 3, 78
Cure, of schizophrenia, *see* Schizophrenia

D

Day, Beth, 3
Decathexis, 27, 30-31
 of Adult, *see* Adult ego state, decathexis of
 of Parent, *see* Parent ego state, decathexis of
Depression, *see* Pathological structures
Developmental stages, 14, 34-48, 49
 adolescence, 45-46
 birth, 35
 eight- to twelve-year-olds, 44-45
 The Fearful Fours, 42-43
 first six months, 35-37
 See also Third order structure
 five- to eight-year-olds, 43-44
 later infancy, 38-39
 mid-infancy, 37-38
 pre-natal, 34-35
 problems with, 47-48
 The Terrible Twos, 39-41
 The Trusting Threes, 41
 young adulthood, 46
Diagnosis, 72-73
 use of categories, 3, 73
Discomfort, 24, 59, 102-103
 shifts in, 65-66
Discounting, 2, 5, 10, 14-18, 55, 57
 classification of, 14-15
 definition, 14
 in games, 17
 table, 16
 and thinking, 17
 treatment, *see* Treatment, discounting
 relationship between types and modes, 15-16
 relationship to redefining, *see* Redefining, internal mechanism
 types of, 14-17, 57
Doing nothing, 10-11
Dreams, 42
Drugs, *see* Medication

E

Ego states, 23-31
 cathexis, 26
 characteristics of, 23-24
 contamination, *see* Contaminations
 development and incorporation of, 24-26, 43, 86
 decathexis, *see* Decathexis
 energy distribution, 26
 exclusion, *see* Exclusion

in frame of reference, 49, 51, 52
redefining, 58, 59
structure of, in regressions, *see* Regression
symbiosis and, 5, 7-9, 60-65
third order structure, 24, 25
Eight- to twelve-year-olds, *see* Developmental stages
Ernst, Franklin H., Jr., 60
Escalations, 20-21
Exclusions, 8, 17, 27, 29-30, 53, 59
of Adult, 93
of Parent, 93
in symbiosis, 60-65
External structure, 1

F

Fantasy, 21-22, 37, 42, 75
Fear, 42, 79-80, 85, 86, 87
The Fearful Fours, *see* Developmental stages
Feelings, 76
dealing with, 40
shifts in, 12, 65, 101
Feeding problems, 36
Five- to eight-year-olds, *see* Developmental stages
Fixations, early, 47-48
Frame of reference, 4, 14, 18, 33, 49-54
in communication, *see* Communication
competitive, 19, 73-74
definition, 49
disagreement between, 63, 64
ego stage function within, 26, 51, 52
internal, 19
nonconventional, 53-54
nonpsychotic, 74
pathological, 53
psychotic, 74-75
structure and function, 50-51
treatment, *see* Treatment, frame of reference
Fully supported regression, *see* Regressive techniques

G

Games, 14, 17, 22, 24, 41, 55, 61, 73-74, 102
discounting in, 14
escalations in, 20-21
frame of reference in, 53
payoff level, 21
positions in, levels of, 66-68
symbiosis in, 6-7
Grandiosity, 2, 5, 10, 47, 55, 57
definition, 18
functions of, 18-19
relationship to redefining, *see* Redefining, internal mechanism
Grief, 37, 39, 86
Guilt, 38, 74, 80, 81

H

Hard Worker, *see* Redefining, roles
Healthy functioning, 5, 19
energy distribution, 26-27
Hebephrenia, *see* Pathological structures
Hexagon, *see* Redefining, hexagon
Hysteria, *see* Pathological structures

I

Inadequate personality, *see* Pathological structures
Incapacitation or violence, 8, 10, 13-14
Intervention, definition, 103
See also Treatment
Intimacy, 6, 19, 33, 45

K

Karpman Drama Triangle, 14, 54, 62, 63, 64, 80

L

Latency stage, *see* Developmental stages, eight- to twelve-year-olds
Little Professor, 21, 37, 41
  A_1, 8-9, 24, 41, 86

M

Manic depressive, *see* Pathological structures
Medication, 76, 99
Memory, 21, 37, 42
Mental health, 6
Modes of discounting, 14-17, 57
Motivation, 51
  for redefining, 56

N

Negative strokes, *see* Strokes

O

Obsessive compulsive, *see* Pathological structures
Oedipal stage, *see* Developmental stages, five- to eight-year-olds
OKness, 3, 33, 34, 36, 52, 76, 81
  competition for, 74
Options, 6, 14-17, 30, 44, 53, 84, 97, 100
  script, 50
  in symbiosis, 55
Oral stage, 33, 80, 82
  See also Developmental stages, first six months, mid-infancy, later infancy

Outpatient structure, 4, 88-89, 96
Overadaptation, 10, 11, 38, 41, 77, 81, 82
Overdetailing, 20
Overgeneralizing, 20

P

Paranoia, *see* Pathological structures
Parent ego state, 21, 23-24, 25-26
  "caging," *see* Reparenting
  decathexis of, 1, 30-31, 88-89
    motivation for, 89
    in regressions, 90
  exclusion of, 29, 93
  in frame of reference, 26, 52
  incorporation of, 43, 44, 86
Parenting, 32-34, 90
  function of, 32
  mistakes in, 33-34
  responsibilities in, 32-33
  symbiosis in, 32
Parent messages, 32, 33-34
Partially supported regression, *see* Regressive techniques
Passive behaviors, 2, 10-14, 55
  definition, 10
Passivity syndrome, 2, 4, 5-22, 49
  origins of, 5
  problem of, 2
Pathological structures, 4, 49
  catatonia, 78-80
  character disorder, 86
  depression, 85
  hebephrenia, 4, 72-73, 76-78
    hebephrenic resolution, 76
  hysteria, 4, 82-83
  inadequate personality, 86-87
  manic depressive, 4, 9, 83-85
  obsessive compulsive, 4, 85
  paranoia, 4, 80-82
  phobias, 87
  schizophrenia, connected consciousness, 75-76
    See also Schizophrenia

Pathology, 26, 72-87
Personality structures, see Pathological structures
Phobias, see Pathological structures
Positive strokes, see Strokes
Pre-natal stage, see Developmental stages
Problem solving, 6, 10, 33-34, 36, 42, 43, 46, 70, 98, 99
  difficulties with, 14-18, 22, 80
Processes, internal and external, 17, 19, 23, 100
  definition, 19
  integration, early scripting, 35-36, 37, 43
  nonintegration, 74-75
Pseudo-regression, see Regression, types of
Psychotic regression, 96
  See also Regression, types of

R

Reactive environment, see Treatment environment
Reality, 14, 100
  definition, 21, 42, 51, 54, 78
Redecision, 52
Redefining, 4, 21, 54-71
  behaviors with, 65-66
  definition, 54-55
  discounting, 59
  and ego states, 58, 59
  experience of, 56-57
  function of, 56
  game positions in, 66
  Hexagon, 67
  internal mechanism of, 57
  relationships, 60-61, 65
    Child-competitive type, 64-65
    Parent-competitive type, 62-64
    symbiotic type, 61-62
  roles, 66-68

and script, 55, 61
symbiotic basis, 56-57, 59-65
transactions, 57-58
  blocking, 59-65, 66
  levels in, 59-60
  tangential, 58-59, 65
  in treatment, 54, 68-71
Regression, 91-97
  decision in, 92, 93-94
  dynamics of, 91-94
  ego state structures in, 92-93
  physiological component, 76, 92, 94
  process of, 3
  regrowth, rate of, 96
  symbiosis in, 94
  therapeutic techniques, 94-97
  types of, 91
    See also Parent ego state, exclusion of, 29
Regressive techniques, 47, 48, 96
  current use of, 47, 48
  early use of, 2
  nonsupported regression, 95
  supported regression, 95-96
Reparenting, 1, 3
  "caging" the Parent in, 90
  definition, 88-89
  and ego state exclusion, 29, 30
  frame of reference change in, 52
  nonpsychotic applications, 89-90
  symbiosis in, 90
Research, 1-4
Responsibility, 13-14, 98, 102
  parent-child, 32-34, 46
  shift in, 7, 10, 19, 62, 65
Roles, redefining, see Redefining, roles

S

Schiff, Aaron, 1, 2
Schiff, Eric, 2

The Schiff Family, 1, 3
Schiff, Jacqui, 1, 2, 3
Schiff, Moe, 1
Schizophrenia, 2, 3, 74–76
    cure, 3, 4, 23
    frame of reference, nonconventional, *see* Frame of reference
    structure of, 74–76
Schizophrenic structure, 2
Script, 8–9, 14, 21, 36, 41, 44, 47, 56
    options, 50
    redefining and, 55, 61
    redefining roles and, 66–68
    rescripting, 13, 49
    thinking problems, 22
Secret, paranoid, 81
Selection problem, *see* Thinking disorders
Selective rescue, 70
Separation, 37
Social contract, 22, 40
Spontaneity, 6, 19, 33
Staff-patient relationships, vii, 3, 4, 101
Strokes, 6, 13–14, 26, 33, 34, 38, 39, 41, 42, 43, 46, 52, 62, 63, 64, 78–79, 82, 85, 86
Structural analysis, 23
Survival issues, 5–6, 26, 30, 32, 56, 64, 65, 74, 76
Symbiosis, 2, 14
    changes with child's growth, *see* Child development
    competition in, 7, 73
        See also Competition
    competitive, 7–8
    complementary, 7–9
    definition, 5
    exclusions in, 29
    first order, 8
    functional, 8–9
    grandiosity in, 18
    healthy and unhealthy, 6, 73
    and parenting, *see* Parenting, symbiosis in
    positions in, 59–60, 61, 62–65, 68
    redefining, relationship to, *see* Redefining
    in regression, 94
    relationship to games, 7
    in reparenting, 90
    resolution of, 32–48
    second order, 8
    structural, 7–8, 60–65
    treatment options, *see* Treatment, symbiosis
Symbiotic contract, 10, 60

T

Teething, 38, 80
Temporary regression, *see* Regression, types of
The Terrible Twos, *see* Developmental stages
Theory, vii, 1–4
Thinking, 22, 24, 25, 36, 37
    disorders, 2, 6, 10, 19–21, 47, 55, 57, 75
    genesis of, 22, 41
    and grandiosity, 18–19
    relationship to redefining, *see* Redefining, internal mechanism
    effective, 19–20, 41
    fantasy and, 21–22
    shifts in, 65
Third order structure, 24, 25
Transactions, 14, 50–51
    See also Redefining, transactions
Transference, 3, 5, 102
    See also Treatment, power exchanges
Treatment, 1, 49, 54, 55–56, 103
    comfort versus discomfort in, *see* Discomfort
    competition, 73

contracts, 101
discounting, 17-18
ego states, options in, 23-24, 31
escalations, 21
exclusions, use of, 30
frame of reference, 51-54
passive behaviors, 10, 70
   agitation, 12
   incapacitation, 13-14
   overadaptation, 11
   violence, 13
pathological structures, 74-87 *passim*
philosophy, 98-103
power exchanges, 102
redefining mechanism, 70
redefining roles, 71
redefining transactions, 68-69
regression, *see* Regression; Regressive techniques
reparenting in, *see* Reparenting
selective rescue in, *see* Selective rescue
symbiosis, 10, 69-70
use of fantasy, 21-22

Treatment environment, 1-2, 4, 74, 88-89, 95-96, 98, 99-100
   outpatient structure, 89, 96
   reactive environment, 100-101
Treatment structure, *see* Treatment environment
The Trusting Threes, *see* Developmental stages

U

Unconditional strokes, *see* Strokes

V

Violence, *see* Incapacitation or violence

W

Witch Parent, 42, 86
Woeful Righteous, *see* Redefining, roles
Woeful Wrongdoer, *see* Redefining, roles